Better Homes and Gardens®

Mexican
COOK BOOK

© 1977 by Meredith Corporation, Des Moines, Iowa.
All Rights Reserved. Printed in the United States of America.
Large-Format Edition. Second Printing, 1983.
Library of Congress Catalog Card Number: 77-74591
ISBN: 0-696-01030-5

On the cover:
The varied cuisine of Mexico
offers such popular dishes
as *Tamales* with *Picadillo* filling,
Enchiladas Rojas with
Chorizo, and *Arroz con Tomate*
(see index for recipe pages).

**BETTER HOMES AND
GARDENS® BOOKS**
Editorial Director:
  Don Dooley
Executive Editor:
  Gerald Knox
Art Director:
  Ernest Shelton
Assistant Art Director:
  Randall Yontz
Production and
Copy Editor:
  David Kirchner
Food Editor:
  Doris Eby
Mexican Cook Book Editors:
  Nancy Morton,
    Senior Associate
    Food Editor
  Flora Szatkowski,
    Associate Food Editor
Senior Food Editors:
  Sandra Granseth
  Sharyl Heiken
  Elizabeth Strait
Associate Food Editor:
  Diane Nelson
Mexican Cook Book Designer:
  Sheryl Veenschoten
Graphic Designers:
  Faith Berven
  Richard Lewis
  Harijs Priekulis
Consultant:
  Barbara Luckett

Our seal assures you
that every recipe in the
Mexican Cook Book is
endorsed by the Better
Homes and Gardens Test
Kitchen. Each recipe
is tested for family appeal,
practicality, and
deliciousness.

Contents

A Glimpse of Mexico

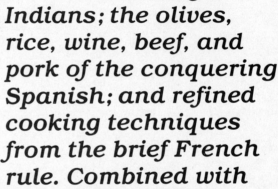

Bursting with color and excitement, Mexican food, like the country itself, reflects a history of many influences. There's the corn, chilies, tomatoes, beans, and squash of the Aztec and Maya Indians; the olives, rice, wine, beef, and pork of the conquering Spanish; and refined cooking techniques from the brief French rule. Combined with modern transportation that defies geographical barriers, all have contributed to the evolution of Mexican food. Such exciting food it is! Discover the heartiness of peasant fare and the refinements of haute cuisine. Experience the startling bite of chilies as well as subtleties apparent only to the aficionado. You'll agree that Mexican food is as rewarding as any in the world.

¡Vámonos!

"Let's go!" Here's what you need to know to start cooking Mexican. To begin with, not every Mexican dish is hot and spicy, but some are. Here you'll find out all about hot chilies—both how to use them and how to modify them to suit your own personal taste.

Next, not everything Mexican is tamales and tortillas, but they are served in some form at almost every meal. You'll enjoy learning to make them from scratch.

And finally, this chapter has descriptions and pictures to acquaint you with ingredients that make Mexican food distinctive, plus recipes for popular fillings and sauces that you'll serve often.

Pictured counterclockwise are *Guacamole*, *Salsa de Chile Rojo*, *Frijoles Refritos*, flour and corn tortillas, and *Salsa Cruda* (see index for page numbers).

Provisiones

Don't get the idea that you can't prepare Mexican food without loading shelves and refrigerator with strange and exotic provisions. Most of the recipes in this book are made with ingredients that can be purchased anywhere in the United States. As a matter of fact, you're already familiar with some of the most important south-of-the-border foods—beans, corn, tomatoes, and peppers, to name a few. But here, and on the next three pages, you can get acquainted with some of the items you may not know. You'll learn what they are, where to buy them, and how to use them.

Beans 1–4

The dried beans that are an essential staple for most Mexicans are much the same as those available in the United States—**garbanzo beans** or **chick peas** (1), **black beans** (2), **kidney beans** (3), and **pinto beans** (4) are among the most popular. Dried beans are usually cooked very slowly and served with their broth (see *Frijoles de Olla,* page 74), or mashed and fried (see *Frijoles Refritos,* page 18). If you can't find these varieties of dried beans at your supermarket, try a health food store. Beans are also available in cans, either cooked or refried.

Corn

Very important in the Mexican diet, corn is eaten in many forms. The most common form is dry corn that has been boiled with lime, then ground to make **masa,** a moist corn dough. Tortillas and tamales are made from masa, although tamale masa is more finely ground. In the United States masa is available in only a few cities, but a dehydrated product, **Masa Harina tortilla flour,** makes very good tortillas and tamales. It is packaged like flour, and can be found in the flour or foreign sections of many supermarkets. **Hominy** is another corn product—boiled dried corn with the hulls removed. Canned hominy is generally available in supermarkets.

Jicama 5

A crisp root vegetable sometimes called the **Mexican potato,** jicama is usually peeled and eaten raw. It's a favorite appetizer when sliced and soaked in lime juice. Jicama can be found in the produce section of Mexican stores and sometimes in large supermarkets.

Tamarind 6

These flavorful pods are used in Mexico to create a distinctive fruity beverage (see *Agua de Tamarindo,* page 91) and a candy. You can find tamarind in specialty stores or large markets.

Tomatillos 7

These little vegetables look like small green tomatoes with papery husks, although their character is very different from ordinary tomatoes. Also called **Mexican green tomatoes, husk tomatoes,** or **ground cherries** in seed catalogs, they can be grown in many North American gardens. Buy them fresh or (more often) canned at Mexican markets. Peel the husk, but not the skin, from fresh tomatillos, or rinse the canned variety before using them.

Tomatoes

Abundant in many Mexican dishes, tomatoes are well-known to Americans. To peel fresh tomatoes, plunge in boiling water for 30 seconds, then cool quickly in cold water; the skins will slip off easily. Fresh and canned tomatoes are plentiful all year.

Pumpkin Seeds 8

Mexicans call these **pepitas,** and frequently use them to thicken gravies and sauces. Toasted pumpkin seeds are a delicious snack. They are available both shelled and in the shell at health food stores and some supermarkets.

Nopales 9

Also known as **nopalitos,** these are the pads of the nopal cactus eaten by Mexicans as a vegetable. To use the fresh cactus pads, scrape off the thorns, but do not peel. Cut in small pieces and cook in boiling salted water till tender; then rinse briefly. Purchase these—fresh, canned, or pickled—in supermarkets or Mexican shops.

Piloncillo 10

This dark brown sugar is formed into hard cones. To use the sugar, grate or shave with a knife or vegetable peeler. Available in Mexican markets, it is easily replaced by dark brown sugar.

Mexican Chocolate

Used for making a frothy hot beverage, Mexican chocolate is usually sold in cylindrical boxes containing tablets of sweetened chocolate, often flavored with cinnamon, almonds, and vanilla. Buy the chocolate at Mexican shops or make your own spicy beverage (see page 91).

Chorizo

This highly seasoned Mexican or Spanish sausage is sold in some parts of the Southwest, but you can make your own if it's not available in your area (see page 18). Otherwise, substitute Italian sausage—still delicious although with a quite different flavor. Canned chorizo is also sold in Mexican specialty shops.

Coriander

The leaves and dried seeds of this plant are used extensively in Mexican cooking. The fresh leaf, known as **cilantro, fresh coriander,** or **Chinese parsley,** resembles parsley in appearance, though the taste is very different. Look for it in the produce section of grocery stores or in Mexican and Oriental shops. **Coriander seed** is the dried seed of the same plant, but has a different character from the fresh. Found in the spice section of supermarkets, the seed has a mild flavor that is equally good in main dishes and sweets.

Cumin

Cumin or **comino seed** is another of Mexico's favorite seasonings. It also is found with the spices in most grocery stores.

Epazote

A popular herb in Mexico, epazote is especially favored in Yucatan, where it's sometimes used as an herbal tea but more often as a seasoning for black beans. You can occasionally buy fresh leaves in Mexican shops, but the dried herb is found in larger grocery stores. Its flavor is subtle, so omit it if you can't find it.

Annatto Seed

Mexicans call this seed **achiote**. Used for subtle flavoring qualities, it also imparts a golden-yellow color to food. Annatto seed is available in spice sections of supermarkets. To use it, crush fine with a mortar and pestle. If the seeds are very hard, simmer them in water for a few minutes, then soak till cool before crushing.

Chiles

No discussion of Mexican food could go far without the mention of chilies. These pungent vegetables characterize much of the food of their native Mexico. Although chilies are notorious for their "hotness," in small doses they can add delicate flavor to food, and many are mild, even sweet.

The chilies illustrated on the opposite page are only a few of the dozens of Mexican varieties. Their many names and aliases are made even more confusing by the natural cross-pollinating that occurs, making ever-different strains of chilies commonplace. The availability of chilies in the United States is not dependable, but you may find most varieties fresh, dried, or canned in Mexican specialty stores and many larger supermarkets. If you can't find a particular chili, don't despair. There are readily available substitutes such as chili powder, crushed red pepper, bottled hot pepper sauce, and cayenne.

How to Prepare Chilies

Be very careful when you handle any kind of chili. They contain oils which can burn your skin and especially your eyes. Avoid direct contact as much as possible. Many cooks wear rubber gloves while handling chilies. In any case, after you have worked with them *be sure to wash hands and nails thoroughly with soap and water.*

To prepare *dried ancho* and *pasilla chilies,* first rinse them well in cold water. Cut the chilies open; discard stems and seeds. Cut chilies in small pieces with scissors or a knife. Place them in a bowl and cover with boiling water. Let stand 45 to 60 minutes to soften. Drain off the water.

Most often you'll buy green chilies *(poblano, California, jalapeño,* and *serrano)* in a can, plain or pickled. To use them, rinse well with cold water and cut open. Hold the chilies with a fork and use a knife to scrape out the seeds and fleshy veins. Then chop or slice the chilies as directed in the specific recipe.

When you can buy fresh green chilies, it is often desirable to remove the skin. To peel fresh green chilies *(poblano, California,* and *bell),* broil them 2 inches from the heat for about 15 minutes, turning often, till they are blistered on all sides. Place the hot peppers in a paper or plastic bag. Close the bag and let stand for 10 minutes or till the peppers are cool enough to handle. The peel should now come off easily and the peppers can be seeded, then stuffed or chopped.

Be sure to cautiously taste each chili before you add it to a dish. Hotness can vary immensely within a variety, even for chilies from the same plant. If a chili is too hot you can use less of it. If it's not hot enough, add a few of the seeds (which are usually the hottest part of the chili) or add as much cayenne, bottled hot pepper sauce, or crushed red pepper as you like.

Ancho Chilies 1

This is the dried poblano chili, and the most commonly used of the dried chilies. It is 3 to 5 inches long and deep brownish-red in color. Its flavor is rich and mildly hot. If ancho chilies are not available, substitute one pasilla chili, 1/4 teaspoon crushed red pepper, *or* about 2 teaspoons chili powder for each chili.

Pasilla Chilies 2

A dry chili that is longer, slimmer, and darker in color than the ancho, the pasilla chili is also slightly hotter. Substitute the same as for ancho chilies.

Pequin Chilies 3

Tiny, dried red chilies that are very hot, pequin (or **tepin**) chilies are usually available in jars or packets in the supermarket spice section. To use, simply crush. Substitute an equal measure of crushed red pepper for pequin chilies.

Green Bell Peppers 4

Familiar to most Americans, these mild sweet peppers are used extensively both north and south of the border. Bell peppers turn red as they ripen, becoming even sweeter. The green ones can be found year-round in grocery stores.

California Chilies 5

Often simply referred to as **green chilies,** fresh California chilies are very popular on the west coast of the United States. They are available canned in most American supermarkets. California chilies vary from mildly hot to hot, and add a special flavor to many traditional Mexican foods.

Serrano Chilies 6

These very hot little chilies are green when fresh, ripening to bright red. About 1 1/2 inches long, they are most commonly used fresh or pickled *(en escabeche).* Buy them pickled in most large supermarkets, or substitute jalapeño chilies.

Jalapeño Chilies 7

Also extremely hot, green jalapeño chilies are about 2 1/2 inches long. They are often available fresh, but you can usually find them canned or pickled *(en escabeche)* in the grocery store.

Poblano Chilies 8

The fresh form of the ancho chili, the poblano chili is usually mild. Similar in size and flavor to bell peppers, fresh poblano chilies are available in the West. The canned variety is more widely distributed. Use bell peppers as a substitute.

Chili Powder 9

In Mexican markets, chili powder is simply a powdered form of ancho, pasilla, or other dried red pepper; however the domestic variety contains extra seasonings such as cumin, oregano, and garlic. American chili powder can substitute for dried ancho and pasilla chilies, but the added spices change the character of the dish (use about 2 teaspoons for each ancho or pasilla chili). Look for American-style chili powder with the spices in most supermarkets.

Cayenne

The ground form of very hot chili peppers, this orange-colored powder is widely available in the spice section of most grocery stores. Use sparingly to add extra hotness.

Crushed Red Pepper 10

This widely marketed product is simply a dried hot red pepper that has been crushed (you may have seen it on the table at Italian restaurants). Since it includes the seeds, it is very hot. Although color and flavor will not be the same as when ancho or pasilla chilies are used, crushed red pepper is a good hotness substitute; use 1/4 teaspoon for each ancho or pasilla chili. You can find crushed red pepper at almost all food stores.

Hot Pepper Sauce 11

This is a liquid form of chilies made by combining the pulp of hot chilies with vinegar and salt. Hot pepper sauce is a convenient way to add hotness at the table. Available in bottles, find it on the condiment shelf at the grocery store.

Tortillas

Tortillas—plain, buttered, or wrapped around a variety of fillings—are found on Mexican tables at nearly every meal. In the corn-producing regions of the South, tortillas are usually made from corn; however, in the northern areas where wheat is grown, flour tortillas are favored. Tortilla "factories" which sell fresh tortillas are found throughout Mexico and even in some United States cities. Since Mexican food has become so popular north of the border, frozen corn and flour tortillas and canned corn tortillas are available in most supermarkets. Although these are fine products, why not get the real spirit of Mexico by making your own corn or flour tortillas?

Corn Tortillas

2 cups Masa Harina
   tortilla flour
1 cup water

Combine tortilla flour with water; mix with hands till dough is moist but holds its shape (add more water if needed). Let stand 15 minutes. Divide dough into 12 balls. Dampen dough slightly with water. Using a tortilla press or flat baking dish, press a ball of dough between sheets of waxed paper to a 6-inch round. Carefully peel off top sheet of paper. Place tortilla, paper side up, on hot ungreased griddle or skillet. Gently peel off remaining sheet of paper. Cook about 30 seconds or till edges begin to dry. Turn; cook till surface appears puffy. Repeat with remaining dough. Makes 12 tortillas.

Flour Tortillas

2 cups all-purpose flour
1 teaspoon salt
1 teaspoon baking powder
1 tablespoon lard or shortening
1/2 to 3/4 cup warm water (110°)

In mixing bowl stir together flour, salt, and baking powder. Cut in lard till mixture resembles cornmeal. Add 1/2 cup warm water and mix till dough can be gathered into a ball (if needed, add more water, 1 tablespoon at a time). Let dough rest 15 minutes. Divide dough into 12 portions; shape into balls. On a lightly floured surface, roll each ball to a 7-inch round. Trim uneven edges to make round tortillas. Cook in ungreased skillet over medium heat about 1 1/2 minutes per side or till lightly browned. Makes 12 tortillas.

Dough for corn tortillas should be moist, yet hold its shape. Divide dough into balls and dampen slightly with a little water. Place between two sheets of waxed paper or plastic wrap on a tortilla press, then press to a 6-inch circle.

Or, press each dough ball flat between pieces of waxed paper or plastic wrap using a flat-bottomed baking dish or pie plate. (For flour tortillas, roll out each ball of dough with a rolling pin on a lightly floured surface. Waxed paper is not necessary.)

Carefully peel off top sheet of paper. Place tortilla, paper side up, on a hot, ungreased griddle or skillet. Gently peel off remaining sheet of paper as shown. Cook till edges begin to dry and tortilla is lightly browned. Turn; cook till surface appears puffy. Stack hot tortillas in a napkin-lined basket to keep warm.

How to make taco shells: In heavy skillet heat 1/4 inch cooking oil. Fry each tortilla 10 seconds or till limp. With tongs fold tortilla in half and continue frying, holding edges apart. Cook 1 1/4 to 1 1/2 minutes longer or till crisp, turning once. Drain on paper toweling.
How to soften tortillas for filling: In small skillet heat 2 tablespoons cooking oil. Holding tortilla with tongs, dip each tortilla in the hot oil for 10 seconds or just till limp. Drain on paper toweling. Repeat with remaining tortillas, adding more oil as needed.

Tamales

For Mexican fiestas and special occasions, tamales are a favorite treat. Filled with meat, they make a hearty meal—or stuffed with sweets, they're an irresistible dessert (see page 87). Make them small for snacks or large for a festive meal. Although it's customary to wrap tamales in cornhusks or banana leaves, foil and parchment work well, too. Enjoy the recipes below, then make a few without filling (called blind) to see why Mexicans think tamales are so special.

Tamales

Cornhusks, aluminum foil,
   or parchment
3 cups Masa Harina
   tortilla flour
2 cups warm water
1 cup lard *or* shortening
1 teaspoon salt
½ recipe (2 cups) Picadillo
   (see page 18)

Prepare tamale wrappers as described on opposite page. Mix together tortilla flour and water; cover and let stand 20 minutes. In large mixer bowl beat together lard and salt till fluffy; beat in flour mixture till well combined.

Measure 2 tablespoons dough onto each tamale wrapper; spread to a 5x3-inch rectangle. Spoon 1 scant tablespoon Picadillo onto dough. Roll up; tie ends.

Place tamales on rack in steamer or electric skillet. Add water to just below rack level. Bring to boiling; cover and steam for 40 to 45 minutes or till tamale pulls away from wrapper, adding water as needed. Makes 26 to 28.

Tamales de Elote   *Fresh Corn Tamales*

6 ears fresh corn on the cob with
   husks
3 cups Masa Harina
   tortilla flour
1 cup lard *or* shortening
2 tablespoons sugar
1 teaspoon baking powder
1 teaspoon salt
2 cups shredded monterey jack
   cheese (8 ounces)
1 4-ounce can green chili
   peppers, rinsed, seeded, and
   chopped

Cut husks from corn. Wash husks; soak in warm water for 30 minutes. Drain. Meanwhile, cut off corn kernels; scrape cobs. Grind corn in food grinder or finely chop in blender. Measure corn; add water to make 2½ cups. Combine with tortilla flour; mix well. Cover and let stand 20 minutes. In large mixer bowl cream lard, sugar, baking powder, and salt till fluffy. Beat in corn mixture.

Measure 2 tablespoons dough onto each tamale wrapper; spread to a 5x3-inch rectangle. Place about 1 tablespoon cheese and ½ teaspoon chopped chili pepper on dough; roll up. (To cover dough, overwrap with soaked dried cornhusks, foil, or parchment, if needed.) Tie wrapper ends with cornhusk or string. Place tamales on rack in large steamer or electric skillet. Add water to just below rack level. Cover; steam 35 to 40 minutes or till tamale pulls away from wrapper, adding water as needed. Makes 36 tamales.

Soak cornhusks in warm water several hours or overnight to soften. Pat with paper toweling to remove excess moisture. (Or use 8x6-inch squares of foil or parchment.) Measure dough onto wrapper. With spatula or wet fingers spread dough to desired size, placing one long edge of dough at one edge of wrapper with equal space at the ends as shown.

Spoon desired filling along dough about one inch in from the even long edges, bringing the filling out to both ends.

Roll tamale jelly-roll fashion starting with the edge nearest filling, being sure to make a tight roll. Tie ends securely with pieces of cornhusk or string. (For foil, fold ends under or twist ends to seal.)

Place tamales on a rack in a large steamer or electric skillet. Add water to just below rack level; bring to boiling. Cover and steam over medium heat till tamale pulls away from wrapper, adding more water as needed. If desired, wrap cooked tamales in moisture-vapor proof material; freeze. To reheat, remove moisture-vapor proof wrap and steam again just till tamales are heated through.

Salsas

Salsa de Chile Rojo Red Chili Sauce (photo on page 6)

4 dried ancho *or* pasilla chilies, *or*
   3 tablespoons chili powder, *or*
   1 teaspoon crushed red
   pepper
4 medium tomatoes (1¹/₂ pounds)
   or 1 15-ounce can tomato
   puree
1 medium onion, cut up
1 clove garlic, minced
1 teaspoon salt
¹/₄ teaspoon sugar
1 tablespoon cooking oil

Cut chilies open. Discard stems and seeds. Cut chilies into small pieces with scissors or a knife. Place in bowl; cover with boiling water. Let stand 45 to 60 minutes. Drain.

To peel tomatoes, dip them in boiling water for 30 seconds; plunge into cold water. Slip skins off. Quarter tomatoes. Place in blender container; cover and blend till nearly smooth. Measure 2 cups of the blended tomatoes; return to blender container (or place canned tomato puree in blender container). Add the drained chilies or chili powder or crushed red pepper. Add onion, garlic, salt, and sugar; cover and blend till smooth.

In 1¹/₂-quart saucepan combine tomato mixture and cooking oil. Cook and stir over medium heat about 10 minutes or till sauce is slightly thickened. Makes 2 cups.

Salsa de Chile Verde Green Chili Sauce

1 medium tomato, peeled and cut
   up
1 4-ounce can green chili
   peppers, rinsed and seeded
1 small onion, cut up
1 clove garlic
1 to 2 tablespoons snipped
   cilantro *or* parsley
1 tablespoon olive oil *or* cooking
   oil
¹/₂ teaspoon salt
   Dash pepper

In blender container combine tomato, chili peppers, onion, garlic, cilantro or parsley, oil, salt, and pepper. Cover and blend till nearly smooth. Pour into small saucepan; bring to boiling. Reduce heat; cook and stir over medium heat about 5 minutes or till slightly thickened. Makes 1 cup.

Sauces Without a Blender

Imagine a woman kneeling over a stone slab grinding the ingredients to make *Salsa de Chile Rojo* with a stone. That's how sauces were made years ago, and that's how they're made today in some Mexican homes. But in modern Mexico, the electric blender has made this process a lot less grinding. Even if you don't have a blender, there are other ways to simplify the preparation of Mexican food.

Most of the sauces on these two pages and throughout the book are based on avocados, tomatoes or tomatillos, chilies, onions, and garlic. Instead of blending those ingredients till smooth, you can first chop them finely, then beat them together with an electric mixer or by hand. Many people prefer the chunkier sauce this method produces, but if you want a smoother consistency, force the mixture through a sieve or food mill. You'll still save plenty of time!

Guacamole Avocado Sauce (photo on page 6)

2 medium avocados, seeded,
    peeled, and cut up
1/2 small onion, cut up
2 tablespoons lemon juice
1 clove garlic, minced
1/2 teaspoon salt
1/4 teaspoon pepper

In blender container place avocados, onion, lemon juice, garlic, salt, and pepper; cover and blend till well combined. Use as a dip for chips or as a sauce to serve with main dishes. Makes about 1 1/4 cups.

Guacamole con Chiles Avocado Sauce with Chilies

2 large avocados, seeded, peeled,
    and cut up
1 small tomato, peeled and cut up
1/2 small onion, cut up
2 or 3 canned green chili peppers,
    rinsed and seeded
2 tablespoons lemon juice
3/4 teaspoon salt

In blender container place avocados, tomato, onion, chili peppers, lemon juice, and salt; cover and blend till well combined. Use as a dip for chips or as a sauce to serve with tacos. Makes about 2 cups.

Salsa Cruda Fresh Tomato Sauce (photo on page 7)

4 medium tomatoes (1 1/2 pounds)
1/2 cup finely chopped onion
1/2 cup finely chopped celery
1/4 cup finely chopped green bell
    pepper
1/4 cup olive oil *or* cooking oil
2 to 3 tablespoons finely chopped
    canned green chili peppers
2 tablespoons red wine vinegar
1 teaspoon mustard seed
1 teaspoon coriander seed,
    crushed
1 teaspoon salt
Dash pepper

To peel tomatoes, dip them in boiling water for 30 seconds; plunge into cold water. Slip skins off; chop tomatoes. Combine chopped tomatoes with onion, celery, green bell pepper, olive or cooking oil, green chili peppers, vinegar, mustard seed, coriander seed, salt, and pepper. Cover; refrigerate several hours or overnight, stirring occasionally. Serve as a relish. Makes about 3 cups.

Salsa Tomato Sauce

1 16-ounce can tomatoes, drained
    and finely chopped
1 4-ounce can green chili
    peppers, rinsed, seeded, and
    chopped
1/2 cup finely chopped onion
1 tablespoon vinegar
1 teaspoon sugar
1/8 teaspoon salt

In mixing bowl thoroughly combine tomatoes, chili peppers, and onion; stir in vinegar, sugar, and salt. Let mixture stand at least 30 minutes at room temperature. Store in refrigerator. Serve as a relish. Makes about 1 cup.

Rellenos *Fillings*

Chorizo *Spicy Sausage*

About 20 feet pork *or* beef
    sausage casings (optional)
1$\frac{1}{3}$ cups water
  $\frac{2}{3}$ cup white vinegar
  2 tablespoons paprika
  5 teaspoons salt
  4 teaspoons crushed red pepper
  1 tablespoon dried oregano
  5 cloves garlic, minced
  1 teaspoon coriander seed
  1 teaspoon ground cumin
  1 teaspoon whole peppercorns
  6 whole cloves
  5 pounds untrimmed boneless
    pork shoulder, cut in 1$\frac{1}{2}$-inch
    cubes
12 ounces pork fat

Rinse sausage casings; soak in water at least 2 hours or overnight. In blender container combine the 1$\frac{1}{3}$ cups water, vinegar, paprika, salt, crushed red pepper, oregano, garlic, coriander, cumin, peppercorns, and cloves. Cover; blend till spices are ground. (Or, in mortar and pestle, grind crushed red pepper, oregano, garlic, coriander, cumin, peppercorns, and cloves. Slowly add water, vinegar, paprika, and salt; mix well.)

With the coarse blade of meat grinder, grind together untrimmed pork and the 12 ounces of pork fat. Add the seasoning mixture; mix well. Grind again. Use as bulk sausage *or* attach sausage stuffer attachment to grinder. Using one 3- to 4-foot piece of casing at a time, push casing onto stuffer, letting some extend beyond end of attachment. Using coarse plate of grinder, grind mixture together, allowing it to fill the casing. Fill casing till firm but not too full, tying with string or twisting when links are 4 to 5 inches long. Wrap and store in the refrigerator 3 to 5 days or in the freezer up to one month. Makes 6$\frac{1}{2}$ pounds.

To cook sausage links: Do not prick. Place links in cold skillet. Add $\frac{1}{4}$ cup *cold water.* Cover and cook slowly for 5 minutes; drain well. Uncover and cook slowly 12 to 15 minutes longer, turning occasionally with tongs.

Frijoles Refritos *Refried Beans (photo on page 6)*

1 pound dry pinto beans (2$\frac{1}{2}$ cups)
6 cups water
$\frac{1}{4}$ cup lard *or* bacon
  drippings
1$\frac{1}{2}$ teaspoons salt
1 clove garlic, crushed

In a 3-quart covered saucepan bring beans and water to boiling. Simmer for 2$\frac{1}{2}$ to 3 hours or till beans are very tender. In a large heavy skillet melt lard; add beans with liquid, salt, and garlic. Mash beans completely. Cook, uncovered, over medium heat about 10 minutes or till thick, stirring often. Serve as a side dish or use as a filling for Burritos (see page 44). Makes about 4$\frac{1}{2}$ cups.

Picadillo *Mexican Hash*

1 pound ground beef
$\frac{1}{2}$ cup chopped onion
1 clove garlic, minced
1 10$\frac{1}{2}$-ounce can tomato puree
1 medium apple, peeled, cored,
  and chopped
$\frac{1}{2}$ cup raisins
$\frac{1}{4}$ cup snipped parsley
$\frac{1}{4}$ cup chopped toasted almonds
1 tablespoon vinegar
1 teaspoon sugar
1 teaspoon salt
$\frac{1}{4}$ teaspoon ground cinnamon
$\frac{1}{4}$ teaspoon ground cumin
$\frac{1}{8}$ teaspoon pepper

In 10-inch skillet cook ground beef, onion, and garlic till meat is brown and onion is tender. Drain off excess fat. Stir in remaining ingredients. Cover; simmer 20 to 25 minutes. Serve as a main dish or use as a filling for tacos or Empanaditas (see page 26). Makes 4 cups.

Fill *Tamales* with *Picadillo*, *Enchiladas Rojas* with *Chorizo*, and serve with *Arroz con Tomate* (see index for pages).

Menu Planning

It's easy to plan menus with Mexican foods. Their variety offers many opportunities to find exactly the character of meal you like. Just use a Mexican dish in an American menu or try one of Mexico's traditional meals.

Mexicans eat as many as five meals a day. Usually the day begins with **desayuno,** an early breakfast of rolls and coffee. Later in the morning comes **almuerzo,** the main breakfast or brunch, which might consist of eggs with meat, bread, beans, and fresh fruit.

The most elaborate and filling meal of the day is eaten in mid-afternoon. **Comida** often entails several courses—appetizer, soup, **sopa seca** (a starchy casserole), fish, main course, salad or vegetable, beans, dessert, and coffee. Occasionally all the courses are served, but less frequently now as businesses eliminate the **siesta** (for after such a meal, there's no choice but to nap).

Late afternoon or early evening brings a meal called **merienda,** either rolls and chocolate or a light snack. As late as midnight, **cena** is served. Lighter than **comida,** it consists of the same elements, though it may be as simple as soup, bread, and dessert.

Don't confine your Mexican cooking to traditional menus, however. Show off **antojitos** at a cocktail party, serve Mexican soups with Yankee sandwiches, present Mexican-style beans at your next barbecue, or finish a meal with a tropical pudding. Imagination is the only limit to what you can do, so be creative!

Turkey Dinner

Mole Poblano de Guajolote 59
Turkey Mole Puebla-Style

Frijoles de Olla 74
Beans in a Pot

Cooked Carrots   Sliced Tomatoes

Tortillas 12

Postre de Virrey 84
Viceroy's Dessert

Coffee

Cena

Sopa de Fideos 33
Vermicelli Soup

Tortilla a la Mexicana 66
Mexican Omelet with Chicken

Bolillos 80 **or** *Tortillas 12*
Spindle Rolls

Atole 91
Hot Cornmeal Beverage

Fresh Fruit

Almuerzo

Huevos Revueltos con Calabacitas 68
Scrambled Eggs with Zucchini
or
Huevos Girasol 66
Sunflower Eggs

Frijoles Blancos 72
White Beans

Bizcochos 81
Egg Biscuits

Coffee

Orange Juice or Fresh Pineapple

Fish Buffet

Pescado a la Naranja 60
Fish in Orange Juice

Budin de Elote 74
Corn Pudding

Ensalada de Ejotes 77
Green Bean Salad

Bolillos 80
Spindle Rolls

Empanadas 81
Dessert Turnovers

Tea or White Wine

Comida

Ceviche 29
Marinated Raw Fish

Sopa de Zanahoria 36
Carrot Soup
or
Sopa de Aguacate 37
Avocado Soup

Sopa Seca de Tortilla 72
Tortilla Casserole

Pollo Almendrado Rojo 56
Red Chicken with Almonds
or
Chuletas de Puerco Adobadas 53
Pork Chops in Adobo Sauce

Ensalada de Calabacita 77
Zucchini Salad
or
Ensalada de Jícama 77
Jicama Salad

Frijoles de Olla 74
Beans in a Pot

Almendrado 84
Almond Pudding with Custard Sauce

Café de Olla 91 **or Coffee**
Pot Coffee

Merienda

Tacos de Queso 40
Cheese Tacos

Frijoles Refritos 18
Refried Beans

Agua de Tamarindo 91
Tamarind Water

Sopapillas 83
Fried Biscuit Puffs

Fiesta Dinner

Chiles Rellenos 69 **or** *Tamales 14*
Stuffed Chilies

Ensalada de Noche Buena 76
Christmas Eve Salad

Buñuelos 83
Fried Sugar Tortillas

Chocolate Mexicano 91
Mexican Hot Chocolate

Antojitos y Sopas

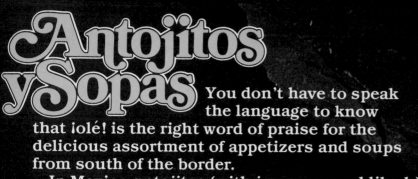

You don't have to speak the language to know that ¡olé! is the right word of praise for the delicious assortment of appetizers and soups from south of the border.

In Mexico *antojitos* (with *j* pronounced like *h*) means "little whims," an apt description for the versatile snacks and tidbits in this chapter. Make them bite-sized for parties and to serve before dinner. Or, choose something more substantial to fend off hunger between meals.

While *sopas* translates simply as soups, their variety and sophistication rival those from anywhere in the world. Even the homey versions are beautiful, with rich, slow-simmered broths made bright by colorful vegetables. Here, too, are subtly seasoned creations, smooth in texture and delicate in color, to serve as a first course or with a luncheon.

Shown clockwise are radish-topped *Gorditas*, crisp and cheesy *Nachos*, boat-shaped *Chalupas*, and *Picadillo*-filled *Empanaditas* (see index for page numbers).

Antojitos *Appetizers and Snacks*

Queso Relleno *Stuffed Cheese*

1 2-pound edam cheese
1/2 pound ground pork
1/4 cup finely chopped onion
2 cloves garlic, minced
1 8-ounce can tomatoes, cut up
1/4 cup chopped pimiento-stuffed
    olives
1/2 teaspoon salt
1/4 teaspoon dried oregano,
    crushed
1/8 teaspoon pepper
1/8 teaspoon ground allspice
1/8 teaspoon ground cinnamon
    Cooking oil
1/4 cup finely chopped green bell
    pepper
2 tablespoons finely chopped
    onion
1 tablespoon cooking oil
1 tablespoon all-purpose flour
1 teaspoon instant beef bouillon
    granules
1/2 cup water
1 tablespoon capers (optional)
12 to 16 6-inch tortillas, heated

With a vegetable peeler remove all red skin from the cheese. Cut a thin slice from the top. Using a grapefruit knife and spoon hollow out the cheese, leaving a shell 1/2 inch thick. Reserve the scooped-out cheese for another use. Soak the cheese shell in lukewarm water for 1 hour.

Meanwhile, in skillet cook ground pork with the 1/4 cup onion and garlic till meat is brown and onion is tender. Drain off fat. Stir in *half* the *undrained* tomatoes, the olives, salt, oregano, pepper, allspice, and cinnamon. Simmer, covered, for 2 minutes.

Drain the cheese and dry with paper toweling. Brush the outside of the cheese shell with some cooking oil. Place cheese in a close-fitting casserole dish. Spoon the hot meat mixture into cheese. Bake, uncovered, in 350° oven about 10 minutes or till sides of cheese just begin to melt.

Meanwhile, in small saucepan cook the green pepper and 2 tablespoons onion in 1 tablespoon cooking oil till tender but not brown. Stir in flour and bouillon granules. Add water and remaining *undrained* tomatoes; cook and stir till thickened and bubbly. Stir in capers.

Remove cheese from oven. Pour some of the hot sauce over cheese. Top with cilantro, if desired; serve at once. Scoop portions onto heated tortillas; top with some of the remaining sauce. Makes 12 to 16 appetizer servings.

Chile con Queso *Chili-Cheese Dip*

1/2 cup finely chopped onion
1 tablespoon butter *or* margarine
2 medium tomatoes, peeled,
    seeded, and chopped
1 4-ounce can green chili
    peppers, rinsed, seeded, and
    chopped
1/4 teaspoon salt
1 1/2 cups shredded cheddar cheese
    Milk
    Tortilla chips (see below)
    or corn chips

In medium skillet cook onion in butter or margarine till tender but not brown. Stir in tomatoes, chili peppers, and salt. Simmer, uncovered, for 10 minutes. Add cheese, a little at a time, stirring till cheese is melted. Stir in a little milk if mixture becomes too thick. Serve immediately with tortilla chips or corn chips. Keep warm in fondue pot over low heat. Makes 1 3/4 cups.

Make Your Own Tortilla Chips

Give dips a Mexican flair by serving them with chips made from corn or flour tortillas. Stack tortillas; cut the stack into six wedges. In a heavy saucepan or deep skillet heat 1/2 inch cooking oil or shortening. Fry the tortilla wedges, a few at a time, about 1 minute for corn tortillas (45 seconds for flour tortillas) or till they are crisp and lightly browned. Drain well on paper toweling. If desired, sprinkle the chips lightly with salt.

Here's an intriguing idea for entertaining—stuffed cheese. Let guests help themselves to *Queso Relleno* and warm tortillas. Heat the tortillas as directed in the tip box on page 33.

Aperitivo de Tomate Verde Tomatillo Dip

¹/₂ **cup bottled green taco sauce**
¹/₂ **cup chunk-style peanut butter**
Bottled hot pepper sauce
Tortilla chips (see page 24)

Slowly stir taco sauce into peanut butter; add hot pepper sauce to taste. Serve with tortilla chips. Makes about 1 cup.

Aperitivo de Frijoles Bean Dip

1 **15-ounce can refried beans**
1 **cup dairy sour cream**
3 **to 5 pickled jalapeño peppers, rinsed and seeded**
Tortilla chips (see page 24)

Blend together refried beans and sour cream. Finely chop the jalapeño peppers; mix well with bean mixture. Spoon into serving bowl; garnish with shredded cheddar cheese and sliced green onion, if desired. Serve with tortilla chips. Makes about 2³/₄ cups.

Nachos *Cheese and Chili Chips (photo on page 23)*

Tortilla chips (see page 24) *or* large corn chips
Monterey jack *or* cheddar cheese
Canned green chili peppers, rinsed and seeded

Spread tortilla chips in a single layer on an ovenproof plate or baking sheet. Cut cheese in ³⁄₄x³⁄₄x¹⁄₄-inch pieces. Cut chili peppers in strips. Place a piece of cheese on each chip; top with a strip of chili pepper. Bake in 400° oven 5 minutes or till cheese melts. Serve hot.

Quesadillas *Cheese Turnovers*

6 ounces monterey jack cheese
1 4-ounce can green chili peppers, rinsed and seeded
³⁄₄ cup Frijoles Refritos (see page 18) *or* canned refried beans
12 6-inch tortillas
2 tablespoons cooking oil

Cut cheese into twelve 3x1x¹⁄₄-inch strips. Quarter chili peppers lengthwise. Spread 1 *tablespoon* of the beans on each tortilla. Top each with a piece of cheese and a piece of chili pepper. Fold tortillas in half; secure each with a wooden pick. In skillet heat oil; cook quesadillas, a few at a time, in the hot oil about 2 minutes per side or till lightly browned and cheese is melted. Makes 12.

Empanaditas *Turnovers (photo on page 22)*

2 cups all-purpose flour
1¹⁄₂ teaspoons baking powder
1 teaspoon salt
¹⁄₂ cup shortening *or* lard
Relleno de Pescado *or* Relleno de Legumbres (see below) *or* 1¹⁄₄ cups Picadillo (see page 18)
Fat for frying (optional)
Milk (optional)

Stir together flour, baking powder, and salt. Cut in shortening till mixture resembles cornmeal. Add ¹⁄₃ cup *cold water,* a little at a time, stirring with a fork till dough forms a ball. Divide into 20 parts. On floured surface roll each to a 4-inch circle. Place about 1 tablespoon desired filling on each. Moisten edges with water; fold in half, pressing edges with fork to seal. Fry in 1¹⁄₂ inches hot fat (375°) for 3 minutes or till golden, turning once. Drain on paper toweling. (Or, place on baking sheet; brush with milk. Bake in 425° oven 15 to 18 minutes or till golden.) Makes 20.

Relleno de Pescado *Seafood Filling*

2 3³⁄₄-ounce cans sardines in oil *or* 2 4¹⁄₂-ounce cans shrimp *or* 1 7¹⁄₂-ounce can crab meat
2 hard-cooked eggs, chopped
¹⁄₄ cup sliced green onion
¹⁄₄ cup mayonnaise
1 tablespoon lemon juice
Cayenne

Drain the canned sardines, shrimp, or crab. Remove and discard any bones or cartilage; chop the seafood. Combine with eggs, green onion, mayonnaise, and lemon juice. Season to taste with cayenne and *salt.* Makes about 2¹⁄₂ cups.

Relleno de Legumbres *Vegetable-Cheese Filling*

1 small zucchini
1 large tomato
¹⁄₂ of a 4-ounce can green chili peppers, rinsed, seeded, and chopped
³⁄₄ cup shredded cheddar cheese

Trim ends from zucchini; cook whole zucchini, covered, in small amount of boiling salted water for 10 minutes or till tender. Drain and chop. Peel, seed, and chop tomato; sprinkle with a little *salt.* Combine with zucchini, chili peppers, and cheese. Makes about 2 cups.

Gorditas *Plump Tortillas (photo on page 23)*

2 dried ancho chilies *or* ½
  teaspoon crushed red pepper
1 8-ounce can red kidney beans
1 cup water
1¾ cups Masa Harina
  tortilla flour
¾ teaspoon salt
½ teaspoon baking powder
  Fat for frying
1½ cups Guacamole (see page 17)
  Radish slices

Discard stems and seeds from chilies; cut up chilies. Cover with boiling water; let stand 45 to 60 minutes; drain. In blender container place soaked chilies or crushed red pepper, *undrained* beans, water, and ½ teaspoon *salt*. Cover and blend till smooth. Combine tortilla flour, the ¾ teaspoon salt, and the baking powder. Add bean mixture; mix well. Cover and let stand 15 minutes. Divide dough into 24 parts; pat each to a 2-inch round. In skillet heat ⅛ inch fat. Fry gorditas about 1½ minutes on each side or till crisp. Drain on paper toweling. Top each with *1 tablespoon* Guacamole and a radish slice. Makes 24.

Gorditas de Maiz Molido *Hominy Gorditas*

2 15-ounce cans hominy, drained
1 teaspoon salt
  Fat for frying
1 15-ounce can refried beans
1 cup mashed avocado
1 cup dairy sour cream

In large bowl combine hominy and salt. Mash till consistency of mush. With hands, shape into rounds 1½ inches in diameter and ½ inch thick. In skillet fry gorditas in small amount of hot fat about 1 minute on each side or till golden. Drain on paper toweling. Meanwhile, heat refried beans. Top each gordita with some of the refried beans, avocado, and sour cream. Makes about 20.

Chalupas *Appetizer Tarts (photo on page 23)*

2 cups Masa Harina
  tortilla flour
¼ cup all-purpose flour
1 teaspoon salt
1 beaten egg
¼ cup shortening *or* lard, melted
  Fat for frying
  Relleno de Pollo *or* Relleno de
  Chorizo (see below)
½ cup dairy sour cream
½ cup sliced pitted ripe olives

In bowl combine tortilla flour, flour, and salt. Stir in 1 cup *water* and egg. Add shortening; mix well. Work dough with hands till it is moist but holds its shape. Chill. Divide into 32 parts (keep covered to prevent dough from drying out). On well floured surface, roll each part to a 5x3-inch oval or a 4-inch round. Pinch edge with fingers to form a ridge. In saucepan or deep skillet heat ½ inch fat to 375°. Place chalupa in hot fat with ridge down. Cook 30 seconds; turn and cook 30 seconds more or till crisp. Drain on paper toweling. Fill each with Relleno de Pollo or Relleno de Chorizo; top with sour cream and sliced ripe olives. Makes 32.

Relleno de Pollo *Chicken Filling*

1 medium tomato
1 4-ounce can green chili peppers
1 cup chopped cooked chicken
1 teaspoon vinegar

Peel and chop tomato. Rinse chili peppers; discard seeds. Chop chili peppers. Stir together chicken, chopped tomato, chopped peppers, vinegar, and 1 teaspoon *salt*. Chill mixture till ready to use. Makes about 1¾ cups.

Relleno de Chorizo *Chorizo Filling*

1 pound chorizo *or* Italian
  sausage
1 medium tomato
¼ cup grated parmesan cheese

Remove sausage casings. In skillet cook sausage till done, stirring to break up. Drain off fat. Peel, seed, and chop the tomato. Stir into chorizo along with parmesan cheese; heat through. Makes about 2¾ cups.

Jalapeños Rellenos Stuffed Hot Jalapeño Peppers

12 pickled jalapeño peppers
 1 3-ounce package cream cheese, softened
½ cup shredded sharp cheddar cheese (2 ounces)
¼ cup sliced green onion
12 pimiento strips

Rinse and drain jalapeño peppers. Slit lengthwise on one side; remove seeds and veins, leaving stem attached. Beat cream cheese till fluffy. Beat in cheddar cheese and green onion. Stuff each pepper with part of the cheese mixture. Arrange on heatproof serving plate or baking sheet; bake in 350° oven about 10 minutes or till cheese melts. Top each pepper with a pimiento strip. Makes 12.

Ceviche Marinated Raw Fish

 1 pound fresh *or* frozen haddock fillets *or* other fish fillets
 1 cup fresh lime *or* lemon juice
 1 small onion
 2 to 3 pickled serrano peppers, rinsed, seeded, and cut in strips
¼ cup olive oil *or* cooking oil
¾ teaspoon salt
¼ teaspoon dried oregano, crushed
⅛ teaspoon pepper
 2 medium tomatoes

Thaw frozen fish. Cut fish fillets into ½-inch cubes. In a nonmetal bowl cover cubed fish with lime or lemon juice. Cover and refrigerate 4 hours or overnight or till fish is opaque, turning occasionally. Thinly slice the onion; separate into rings. Add to fish with pickled peppers, olive oil or cooking oil, salt, oregano, and pepper. Toss gently to combine well; chill. Peel, seed, and chop tomatoes; toss with chilled fish mixture. Sprinkle with snipped cilantro or parsley, if desired. Makes 10 to 12 appetizer servings.

About this recipe: Also known as *seviche,* this delicate dish gets its characteristic flavor and texture from the lime or lemon juice that "cooks" the fish.

Carnitas Meat Tidbits

1½ pounds boneless pork shoulder
 Garlic salt
 Guacamole *or* Salsa Cruda (see page 17) *or* canned taco sauce
 Warm tortillas (optional)

Cut pork into 1-inch cubes; spread in a 12x7½x2-inch baking dish. Sprinkle lightly with garlic salt and *pepper.* Add *water* to depth of ½ inch. Bake in 350° oven 2 to 2½ hours or till water evaporates and meat is brown. Skewer with wooden picks for dipping into sauce. Or, mix meat and sauce and fill tortillas. Makes 8 to 10 appetizer servings.

Pepitas Toasted Pumpkin Seeds

 2 cups shelled pumpkin seeds
 1 tablespoon cooking oil
 1 teaspoon salt

Combine pumpkin seeds, oil, and salt; spread in a shallow baking pan. Toast in 350° oven for 15 minutes, stirring once or twice. Drain on paper toweling. Store pepitas in a tightly covered container. Makes 2 cups.

Cacahuates Endiablados Deviled Peanuts

 1 pound raw peanuts (3¼ cups)
 1 tablespoon cooking oil
 2 teaspoons chili powder
 1 teaspoon salt
¼ teaspoon cayenne

In mixing bowl combine peanuts, oil, chili powder, salt, and cayenne. Spread in a 13x9x2-inch baking pan. Bake in 350° oven for 30 minutes or till peanuts are lightly browned, shaking pan occasionally. Makes about 3 cups.

Appetizers shown include sophisticated *Ceviche,* fiery *Jalapeños Rellenos,* and crunchy *Pepitas.*

Sopas *Soups*

Sopa de Pollo a la Mexicana *Mexican Chicken Soup*

1 4½- to 5-pound stewing chicken, cut up
6 cups water
3 to 4 onion slices
3 stalks celery, cut up
1 teaspoon salt
⅛ teaspoon pepper
1 16-ounce can tomatoes, cut up
3 medium carrots, thinly sliced (1½ cups)
1 medium onion, chopped (½ cup)
4 teaspoons instant chicken bouillon granules
1 small zucchini, thinly sliced (4 ounces)
1 cup frozen peas
1 small avocado, seeded, peeled, and sliced

In Dutch oven combine chicken, water, onion slices, celery, salt, and pepper. Simmer, covered, for 2 hours or till chicken is tender. Remove chicken from broth. Strain broth, discarding vegetables; return broth to Dutch oven. Add *undrained* tomatoes, sliced carrots, chopped onion, and bouillon granules; simmer, covered, for 30 minutes or until the carrots are tender.

Meanwhile when chicken is cool enough to handle, remove skin and bones from chicken; discard skin and bones. Cube chicken; add to broth along with zucchini and peas. Cover and simmer 10 to 15 minutes longer or till vegetables are tender. Just before serving, garnish with avocado slices. Makes 10 servings.

Sopa de Flan *Custard Soup*

3 eggs
½ cup milk
¼ teaspoon salt
   Dash pepper
   Dash ground nutmeg
2 tablespoons butter *or* margarine
2 tablespoons all-purpose flour
1 10¾-ounce can condensed chicken broth
¾ cup water
½ cup whipping cream
   Salt and pepper

Beat eggs with milk, salt, pepper, and nutmeg. Pour into a buttered 8x4x2-inch loaf pan. Set pan in a larger shallow pan on oven rack. Pour hot water around loaf pan to depth of 1 inch. Bake in 325° oven 25 to 30 minutes or till a knife inserted just off-center comes out clean. Chill; cut custard into small cubes.

Meanwhile, melt butter or margarine; stir in flour. Add condensed chicken broth and water all at once; cook and stir till thickened and bubbly. Stir in cream. Gently stir in cubed custard; heat through. Season to taste with additional salt and pepper. Makes 4 servings.

Caldo Miche *Fish Soup*

1 1½-pound fresh *or* frozen drawn catfish *or* other fish (with head and tail)
6 cups water
1 16-ounce can tomatoes, cut up
2 medium onions, chopped (1 cup)
2 4-ounce cans green chili peppers, rinsed, seeded, and chopped
2 cloves garlic, minced
1 bay leaf
2 teaspoons salt
½ teaspoon dried oregano, crushed
¼ teaspoon pepper

Thaw frozen fish. In large saucepan combine water, *undrained* tomatoes, onions, chili peppers, garlic, bay leaf, salt, oregano, and pepper. Bring to boiling; cover and simmer about 30 minutes till onion is tender. Cut fish in half if necessary to fit saucepan. Add fish to soup; simmer, covered about 15 minutes or till fish flakes easily with a fork. Remove fish; discard head, tail, skin, and bones. Remove bay leaf. Cut fish meat into bite-size pieces; return to soup. Heat through. Garnish with snipped cilantro or parsley, if desired. Makes 8 servings.

You'll never make a heartier, better tasting chicken soup than *Sopa de Pollo a la Mexicana*. Full of delicious vegetables and topped with avocado slices, it's sure to please a hungry group.

Sopa Ranchera Ranch-Style Soup

¼ **cup chopped onion**
1 **tablespoon cooking oil**
4 **cups chicken broth**
¼ **cup long grain rice**
¼ **cup tomato puree**
¼ **teaspoon salt**
   Dash pepper
1 **cup frozen peas**

In saucepan cook onion in hot oil till tender but not brown. Stir in chicken broth, rice, tomato puree, salt, and pepper. Bring to boiling. Reduce heat; cover and simmer for 25 minutes. Stir in frozen peas; simmer, covered, 5 minutes longer. Makes 4 servings.

Sopa de Albóndigas Meatball Soup

1 medium onion, chopped (¹/₂ cup)
1 clove garlic, minced
2 tablespoons cooking oil
4 cups water
2 10¹/₂-ounce cans condensed
   beef broth
1 6-ounce can tomato paste
2 medium potatoes, peeled and
   cubed (2 cups)
2 medium carrots, sliced (1 cup)
1 beaten egg
¹/₄ cup snipped cilantro or parsley
1 teaspoon salt
¹/₂ teaspoon dried oregano,
   crushed
¹/₈ teaspoon pepper
1 pound ground beef
¹/₄ cup long grain rice

In large saucepan cook onion and garlic in hot oil till onion is tender but not brown. Stir in water, broth, and tomato paste. Bring to boiling; add potatoes and carrots. Simmer for 5 minutes.

Meanwhile combine egg, cilantro or parsley, salt, oregano, and pepper. Add ground beef and uncooked rice; mix well. Form mixture into 1-inch meatballs. Add, a few at a time, to the simmering soup. Return soup to boiling; reduce heat and simmer about 30 minutes or till meatballs and vegetables are done. Makes 8 to 10 servings.

Menudo Tripe Soup

2 pounds honeycomb tripe
1 1¹/₂-pound veal knuckle
6 cups water
3 medium onions, chopped (1¹/₂
   cups)
2 cloves garlic, minced
2 teaspoons salt
¹/₂ teaspoon coriander seed
¹/₄ teaspoon dried oregano,
   crushed
¹/₄ teaspoon crushed red pepper
¹/₄ teaspoon pepper
1 15-ounce can hominy
   Pequin chilies or crushed red
   pepper
   Lime wedges

Cut tripe into 1-inch pieces. Place in a Dutch oven with veal knuckle, water, onions, garlic, salt, coriander, oregano, the ¹/₄ teaspoon crushed red pepper, and pepper. Simmer, covered, for 3 hours till tripe has a clear, jellylike appearance and veal is very tender.

Remove veal knuckle from pot. When cool enough to handle, discard bones; chop meat and return to soup. Add *undrained* hominy; cover and simmer 20 minutes longer. Serve with pequin chilies or crushed red pepper to taste. Garnish with lime wedges. Makes 8 to 10 servings.

About this recipe: Widely popular in Mexico, this hearty soup is enjoyed at lunch, supper, and even breakfast. When eaten with plenty of extra hot pepper, it is reputed to cure hangovers. Canned *menudo* is available in many large supermarkets and Mexican stores.

Sopa de Ajo Garlic Soup

6 cloves garlic
1 tablespoon olive or cooking oil
2 10¹/₂-ounce cans condensed
   beef broth
2 cups water
2 sprigs cilantro or parsley
1 bay leaf
2 slices bread
1 tablespoon butter or margarine,
   softened
2 well-beaten egg yolks

With flat side of knife, mash garlic cloves. In large saucepan cook garlic in hot oil till tender. Stir in beef broth, water, cilantro or parsley, and bay leaf. Bring to boiling; reduce heat and simmer, covered, for 40 minutes.

Meanwhile spread bread with softened butter; cut in quarters. Place bread quarters on baking sheet. Bake in 325° oven for 20 minutes or till crisp and lightly browned.

Strain hot soup; discard garlic, cilantro, and bay leaf. Gradually add *1 cup* of the hot soup to beaten yolks, stirring constantly. Return to saucepan; serve at once. Garnish each serving with 2 toast quarters. Makes 4 servings.

Sopa de Albóndigas y Garbanzo *Meatball-Garbanzo Soup*

1 **pound dry garbanzo beans (2¹/₂ cups)**
8 **cups beef broth**
³/₄ **cup finely chopped onion**
¹/₂ **cup chopped green bell pepper**
2 **tablespoons snipped parsley**
1¹/₄ **teaspoons salt**
¹/₄ **teaspoon pepper**
¹/₄ **teaspoon ground coriander seed**
2 **beaten eggs**
1 **tablespoon milk**
³/₄ **cup soft bread crumbs (1 slice)**
  Dash ground cinnamon
  Dash ground nutmeg
1 **pound ground beef**

In Dutch oven combine beans with *4 cups* of the beef broth and 4 cups *water*. Bring to boiling; simmer 2 minutes. Remove from heat; let stand, covered, for 1 hour. Do not drain. Stir in remaining 4 cups beef broth, ¹/₂ *cup* of the chopped onion, the green bell pepper, *1 tablespoon* of the parsley, ¹/₄ *teaspoon* of the salt, ¹/₈ *teaspoon* of the pepper, and the coriander. Bring to boiling; reduce heat and simmer, covered, for 1³/₄ hours.

Meanwhile, combine eggs and milk; add bread crumbs, the remaining ¹/₄ cup onion, 1 tablespoon parsley, 1 teaspoon salt, ¹/₈ teaspoon pepper, the cinnamon, and nutmeg. Add ground beef; mix well. Shape into about 40 meatballs, using 1 tablespoon of the meat mixture for each. Add meatballs to soup; cover and simmer 15 minutes longer or till meatballs are done. Makes 10 servings.

Potaje de Garbanzo *Garbanzo Bean Soup*

1 **pound dry garbanzo beans**
1 **large onion, chopped (1 cup)**
3 **slices bacon, chopped**
1 **bay leaf**
1 **clove garlic, minced**
1 **tablespoon salt**
2 **hard-cooked eggs, chopped**

Soak garbanzo beans in 10 cups *water* overnight. (Or, bring to boiling; boil 2 minutes. Cover and let stand for 1 hour.) Do not drain. Stir in onion, bacon, bay leaf, garlic, salt, and ¹/₄ teaspoon *pepper*. Cover and simmer for 3 to 3¹/₂ hours or till beans are very tender. Remove bay leaf. Mash beans slightly. Garnish with chopped eggs. Makes 8 to 10 servings.

Sopa de Fideos *Vermicelli Soup*

4 **ounces vermicelli**
1 **tablespoon cooking oil**
1 **medium onion, chopped (¹/₂ cup)**
1 **clove garlic, minced**
2 **10¹/₂-ounce cans condensed beef broth**
1 **10¹/₂-ounce can tomato puree**
2 **tablespoons snipped parsley**
  Grated parmesan cheese

Break vermicelli into small pieces (about 2 cups). In a 3-quart saucepan cook vermicelli in oil over low heat till golden brown. Drain and set aside, reserving oil. Cook onion and garlic in reserved oil till onion is tender but not brown. Add beef broth, tomato puree, the browned vermicelli, and 2¹/₂ soup cans (about 3¹/₄ cups) *water*. Simmer, covered, about 25 minutes or till vermicelli is done. Stir in parsley; season to taste with salt and pepper. Sprinkle with parmesan cheese. Makes 6 to 8 servings.

Serve Hot Tortillas

Warm tortillas, plain or buttered, make the perfect accompaniment for any of these soups. The easiest way to heat a large number of tortillas is to wrap a stack of them in foil, then heat in a 325° oven for 10 to 15 minutes. To warm just a few, heat one at a time directly on a hot ungreased griddle, turning often and watching carefully. Wrap heated tortillas in a napkin to keep warm. If the tortillas seem dry, sprinkle them with a little water before reheating.

Caldo de Puerco *Pork Sparerib Soup*

2 pounds pork spareribs, cut in
  half crosswise
8 cups water
3 carrots, sliced
1 turnip, peeled and cubed
1 large onion, chopped
  (1 cup)
2 tablespoons chili powder
1 tablespoon salt
1 clove garlic, minced
1 teaspoon cumin seed
$1/2$ teaspoon aniseed
$1/4$ teaspoon pepper
1 small head cabbage, shredded
  (4 cups)

Cut ribs apart between bones into individual ribs. Sprinkle with a little salt and pepper. Arrange the ribs in a shallow baking pan; bake in 450° oven for 25 minutes or till well browned. Pour off fat.

Transfer the browned ribs to a large saucepan. Add water, carrots, turnip, onion, chili powder, salt, garlic, cumin, aniseed, and pepper. Bring mixture to boiling. Reduce heat; cover and simmer for 2 hours or till meat is very tender. Skim off fat. Stir shredded cabbage into soup; cook 5 minutes longer. Makes 10 to 12 servings.

Sopa de Bolitas de Tortilla *Tortilla-Ball Soup*

7 6-inch corn tortillas, torn
$1/4$ cup milk
1 small onion, cut up
1 clove garlic
1 egg
$1/4$ teaspoon dried epazote,
  crushed (optional)
$1/4$ cup shredded cheddar cheese
  (1 ounce)
$1/2$ teaspoon salt
$1/8$ teaspoon pepper
  Cooking oil
3 cups beef broth
$1/2$ cup light cream
2 tablespoons tomato paste

Soak tortillas in milk about 5 minutes till somewhat softened. Place tortillas and milk in blender container with onion, garlic, egg, and epazote. Cover and blend till smooth.

In bowl combine tortilla mixture with cheese, salt, and pepper. Shape into 18 one-inch balls using about 1 tablespoon of mixture for each. Fry tortilla balls in $1/2$ inch hot oil for about $1^{1}/_{2}$ minutes or till lightly browned, turning once. Drain on paper toweling; keep warm.

In saucepan combine $2^{1}/_{2}$ *cups* of the broth and the cream; heat through. Meanwhile blend remaining $1/2$ cup beef broth with tomato paste. Gradually add to hot mixture. Sprinkle with cilantro leaves, if desired. Add tortilla balls; serve immediately. Makes 6 servings.

Sopa de Tortilla *Tortilla Soup*

1 8-ounce can tomatoes
1 medium onion, cut up
1 clove garlic
2 tablespoons snipped cilantro *or*
  parsley
$1/4$ teaspoon sugar
4 cups chicken broth
6 6-inch tortillas
  Cooking oil
1 cup shredded monterey jack *or*
  longhorn cheese (4 ounces)

In blender container combine *undrained* tomatoes, onion, garlic, cilantro, and sugar. Cover and blend till nearly smooth. Turn into a large saucepan; stir in chicken broth. Bring to boiling; cover and simmer for 20 minutes.

Meanwhile, cut tortillas into $1/2$-inch-wide strips. Fry strips in $1/2$ inch hot oil for 40 to 50 seconds or till crisp and lightly browned. Drain on paper toweling. Divide fried tortilla strips and cheese among soup bowls. Ladle soup over; serve immediately. Makes 4 or 5 servings.

Caldo de Puerco and *Sopa de Bolitas de Tortilla* are two fine reasons that Mexican soups should be more famous.

Sopa de Frijol Negro Black Bean Soup

1 cup dry black beans (6½
   ounces)
6 cups water
4 slices bacon
½ cup chopped onion
1 clove garlic, minced
1 large tomato, chopped
2 teaspoons salt
½ teaspoon dried oregano,
   crushed
¼ teaspoon pequin chilies,
   crushed, or ¼ teaspoon
   crushed red pepper
Dash pepper
⅓ cup dry sherry
Lime or lemon slices

In 3-quart saucepan combine beans and water; soak overnight. (Or, cover and simmer 2 minutes. Remove from heat; cover and let stand 1 hour.) Do not drain. Simmer, covered, for 2½ to 3 hours or till beans are tender.

In small skillet cook bacon till crisp; drain, reserving 2 tablespoons drippings. Crumble bacon; set aside. Cook onion and garlic in reserved drippings till tender. Add to beans along with tomato, salt, oregano, chilies or crushed red pepper, and pepper. Cover; simmer 30 minutes.

Press bean mixture through sieve or process in blender, half at a time, till smooth. Return to saucepan; stir in sherry. Heat through, 5 to 10 minutes. Garnish with bacon and lime or lemon slices. Makes 4 to 6 servings.

Sopa de Lentejas Lentil Soup

1 pound dry lentils (2⅓ cups)
8 cups water
1 16-ounce can tomatoes, cut up
2 slices bacon, chopped
1 medium onion, chopped (½ cup)
1 medium carrot, chopped (½
   cup)
3 tablespoons snipped parsley
2 tablespoons wine vinegar
1 clove garlic, minced
2½ teaspoons salt
½ teaspoon dried oregano, crushed
¼ teaspoon pepper

In kettle or Dutch oven combine lentils with water, undrained tomatoes, bacon, onion, carrot, parsley, vinegar, garlic, salt, oregano, and pepper. Bring to boiling; reduce heat. Cover and simmer for 1½ hours or till lentils and vegetables are tender. Makes 8 to 10 servings.

Sopa de Zanahoria Carrot Soup

4 medium carrots, cut up (2 cups)
½ cup water
2 teaspoons instant chicken
   bouillon granules
½ teaspoon sugar
¼ teaspoon dried mint, crushed
¼ cup chopped onion
1 tablespoon butter or margarine
1 tablespoon all-purpose flour
2½ cups milk
1 3-ounce package cream cheese,
   cubed
½ teaspoon salt
Dash pepper

In covered saucepan cook carrots in water with bouillon granules, sugar, and mint for about 25 minutes or till very tender. Meanwhile, cook onion in butter or margarine till tender but not brown. Stir in flour. Add milk all at once; cook and stir till thickened and bubbly. Gradually add about 1 cup of the hot milk mixture to cream cheese; beat until smooth. Return to saucepan and mix well.

In blender container place carrots with their liquid; cover and blend till smooth. (Or, force through a sieve or food mill.) Add carrot mixture to milk mixture. Cook and stir till soup just comes to boiling. Stir in salt and pepper. Garnish with fresh mint leaves, if desired. Makes 4 servings.

Sopa de Calabacita   Summer Squash Soup

4 cups water
1 pound zucchini *or* summer
   squash, chopped (3 cups)
1 large onion, chopped (1 cup)
2 tablespoons instant chicken
   bouillon granules
2 tablespoons butter *or* margarine
2 tablespoons all-purpose flour
2 slightly beaten egg yolks
1 cup light cream

In saucepan combine water, squash, onion, and chicken bouillon granules. Simmer, covered, about 15 minutes or till squash and onion are very tender. Place half the mixture in blender container; cover and blend till smooth. Repeat with remaining mixture.

In large saucepan melt butter; stir in flour. Add blended zucchini mixture; cook and stir till thickened and bubbly. Stir about 1 cup of the hot mixture into the beaten egg yolks. Return to pan; stir in cream. Heat through, but do not boil. Makes 6 servings.

Sopa de Elote   Corn Soup

6 ears fresh corn
3 medium tomatoes, peeled,
   seeded, and cut up
1/2 cup finely chopped onion
2 tablespoons butter *or* margarine
4 cups beef broth
1/2 cup whipping cream

Cut corn off cob; scrape cobs (should have about 4 cups). In blender container combine *half* the corn and *half* the tomatoes; cover and blend till smooth, scraping sides often. Repeat with remaining corn and tomatoes.

In large saucepan cook onion in butter till tender; add corn mixture and broth. Cover and simmer 10 to 15 minutes. Gradually stir in cream. Heat through but do not boil. Season to taste with salt and pepper. Makes 8 servings.

Sopa de Aguacate   Avocado Soup

2 tablespoons butter *or* margarine
2 tablespoons all-purpose flour
1 13 3/4-ounce can chicken broth
   Few dashes bottled hot pepper
   sauce
1 large avocado
1 cup light cream

In 1 1/2-quart saucepan melt butter; stir in flour. Add chicken broth and hot pepper sauce; cook and stir till thickened and bubbly. Cut avocado in half. Discard seed and peel. In blender container combine avocado pulp and cream. Cover and blend till smooth. Add to mixture in saucepan. Heat through. Season to taste with salt and pepper. Garnish with sliced green onion and additional avocado, if desired. Makes 4 servings.

Gazpacho   Iced Vegetable Soup

6 tomatoes
1 1/2 cups tomato juice
1 medium cucumber, peeled,
   seeded, and chopped
1 medium onion, finely chopped
1 small green bell pepper, finely
   chopped
1 small clove garlic, minced
1/4 cup olive oil *or* cooking oil
2 tablespoons vinegar
1 teaspoon salt
1/8 teaspoon pepper
   Few drops bottled hot pepper
   sauce
   Croutons *or* toasted bread
   cubes

Plunge tomatoes in boiling water for 30 seconds to loosen skins, then immerse in cold water. Slip skins off; coarsely chop tomatoes.

In a large mixing bowl combine the chopped tomatoes, tomato juice, chopped cucumber, onion, green bell pepper, garlic, olive oil or cooking oil, vinegar, salt, pepper, and bottled hot pepper sauce. Chill. If desired, add an ice cube to each serving. Top with croutons or toasted bread cubes. Makes 6 servings.

Platos Mayores

If your acquaintance with
Mexican main dishes is
limited to tacos and enchiladas,
read on! Not only will you find a wealth of colorful
tortilla concoctions, but also some of the tastiest meat,
poultry, fish, and egg dishes you'll ever try.

The tortilla platters start with the trusty cornmeal or flour tortilla,
but the fun begins when fillings and toppings are added. As
the combinations or shapes change, so do
the recipe names, and the resulting variety is endlessly
delicious.

And don't miss Mexico's imaginative beef or pork
stews. Their outstanding flavor comes from
tempting sauces that mingle seasonings,
vegetables, and sometimes fruit. Fish and
poultry, so popular from coast to coast, also
benefit from artful Mexican seasoning and
cooking skill.

And, where there are chickens, there
are plenty of eggs to fry or scramble with
chilies, sausage, and vegetables, or
to turn into tender omelets.

Pictured clockwise are *Mancha Manteles de
Cerdo, Chiles en Nogada* sprinkled with
pomegranate seeds, and egg-topped *Pollo
Borracho* (see index for page numbers).

Platos Mexicanos *Tortilla Specialties*

Enrollados *Fried Enchiladas*

$1/2$ cup chopped onion
$1/4$ cup water
 1 15-ounce can tomato puree
 1 or 2 pickled serrano *or* jalapeño peppers, rinsed, seeded, and chopped
$1/4$ teaspoon salt
 1 pound ground pork
 1 cup chopped onion
 2 medium potatoes, cooked, peeled, and chopped
$1^1/2$ teaspoons salt
 4 egg whites
 4 egg yolks
 1 tablespoon water
 2 tablespoons all-purpose flour
$1/4$ teaspoon salt
 2 tablespoons cooking oil
 12 6-inch tortillas
 Fat for deep-fat frying
 Shredded lettuce
 Shredded cheddar cheese

In covered saucepan cook the $1/2$ cup onion in the $1/4$ cup water about 5 minutes till tender. Stir in $1^1/4$ *cups* of the tomato puree, the chopped peppers, and $1/4$ teaspoon salt. Heat to boiling; simmer, covered, 10 minutes. Uncover; simmer 2 to 3 minutes or till slightly thickened. Set aside.

In skillet cook pork and the 1 cup onion till pork is brown and onion is tender. Drain off fat. Stir in remaining $1/2$ cup tomato puree, the cooked potatoes, and $1^1/2$ teaspoons salt. Heat through. Set filling aside. Beat egg whites till stiff peaks form. Beat egg yolks and 1 tablespoon water slightly. Add flour and $1/4$ teaspoon salt; beat about 3 minutes or till thick and lemon-colored. Fold into whites.

To assemble enrollados, heat 2 tablespoons oil in skillet. Dip each tortilla in the hot oil for 10 seconds or just till limp. Spoon about $1/4$ cup filling onto each tortilla; roll up. Dip filled tortillas in egg mixture, being sure ends are covered. Cook in deep hot fat (375°) about 2 minutes per side or till golden brown. Drain on paper toweling. Reheat sauce. Arrange enrollados on platter; pour sauce over. Garnish with lettuce and cheese. Makes 6 servings.
Alternate directions: Omit the egg batter and deep-fat fry the filled tortillas. Garnish as above.

Tacos de Queso *Cheese Tacos*

 1 medium onion, chopped ($1/2$ cup)
 Cooking oil
 1 16-ounce can tomatoes, cut up
 1 4-ounce can green chili peppers, rinsed, seeded, and chopped
 1 teaspoon dried oregano, crushed
 12 6-inch tortillas
 8 ounces monterey jack *or* longhorn cheese
 1 cup dairy sour cream

Cook onion in *2 tablespoons* oil till tender but not brown. Stir in *undrained* tomatoes, chili peppers, and oregano. Simmer about 20 minutes till very thick.

In skillet dip each tortilla in *2 tablespoons* hot oil about 10 seconds or just till limp. Drain on paper toweling. Cut cheese into 12 strips. Place 1 strip of cheese and 2 tablespoons sauce down center of each tortilla; overlap edges. Arrange on baking sheet, seam side up. Bake, covered, in 350° oven for 8 minutes. Uncover; bake 3 to 4 minutes more. Open tortillas and add sour cream; roll up. Serves 6.

Tacos Con Carne *Tacos with Meat*

 12 taco shells (see page 13) *or* packaged taco shells
 1 pound ground beef *or* bulk pork sausage
 1 medium onion, chopped ($1/2$ cup)
 1 clove garlic, minced
 1 teaspoon chili powder
$3/4$ teaspoon salt
 2 tomatoes, chopped and drained
 Shredded lettuce
 1 cup shredded sharp cheddar cheese (4 ounces)
 Canned taco sauce *or* Salsa de Chile Rojo (see page 16)

Arrange taco shells on a baking sheet lined with paper toweling. Warm in a 250° oven while preparing meat mixture.

In skillet cook beef or pork, onion, and garlic till meat is brown and onion is tender. Drain off fat. Season meat mixture with chili powder and salt. Stuff each of the taco shells with some of the meat mixture, tomatoes, lettuce, and cheese; pass taco sauce. Makes 6 servings.
For soft tacos: Heat fresh, frozen, or canned tortillas, one at a time, in 2 tablespoons hot cooking oil for 10 seconds or just till limp; drain on paper toweling. Fold warm tortillas around meat mixture, tomatoes, lettuce, cheese, and taco sauce.

The colors of the Mexican flag influence many food combinations, too. Here layers of guacamole, sour cream, and chicken in tomato sauce unfurl in *Tacos Verde, Blanco, y Rojo.*

Tacos Verde, Blanco, y Rojo *Green, White, and Red Tacos*

   1 **small onion, chopped**
   1 **tablespoon cooking oil**
   1 **8-ounce can tomato sauce**
   2 **pickled serrano *or* jalapeño peppers, rinsed, seeded, and chopped, *or* 1/2 teaspoon crushed red pepper**
1/4 **teaspoon salt**
   2 **cups chopped cooked chicken *or* pork**
   2 **tablespoons cooking oil**
 12 **6-inch tortillas**
   2 **cups Guacamole (see page 17)**
1/2 **cup dairy sour cream**

Cook onion in the 1 tablespoon oil till tender; stir in tomato sauce, peppers, and salt. Simmer, covered, for 5 minutes. Stir in chicken or pork; heat through. Keep warm.

In small skillet heat the 2 tablespoons oil. Holding tortilla with tongs, dip each tortilla in the hot oil for about 10 seconds or just till limp. Drain on paper toweling. Spoon a little green Guacamole, white sour cream, and red meat mixture on one half of each tortilla. Fold in half over filling; serve immediately. Makes 6 servings.

Tostada Compuesta *Tostada Platter*

1 **pound ground beef**
1/2 **cup chopped onion**
1 **clove garlic, minced**
1/2 **teaspoon chili powder**
1 **8-ounce can cut green beans**
1 **8-ounce can red kidney beans**
  Cooking oil
6 **10-inch flour tortillas**
1 **large tomato, chopped**
1 **small head lettuce, shredded**
1 **cup shredded sharp American
    cheese (4 ounces)**
  Creamy French salad dressing

In skillet cook beef, onion, and garlic till meat is brown and onion is tender. Drain off fat. Add chili powder and 1/2 teaspoon *salt*. Set aside and keep warm. In saucepan combine *undrained* green beans and kidney beans; heat and drain. In heavy skillet heat 1/4 inch cooking oil. Fry tortillas, one at a time, in hot oil for 20 to 40 seconds on each side or till crisp and golden. Drain on paper toweling. Keep warm in foil in 250° oven. Place tortillas in center of dinner plates. Dividing ingredients equally among tortillas, layer ingredients for tostadas in the following order: meat, beans, tomato, lettuce, and cheese. Serve at once. Pass salad dressing. Makes 6 servings.

Tostadas de Jaiba *Crab Tostadas*

  Cooking oil
8 **6-inch tortillas**
1 **tablespoon lime juice**
1 **tablespoon olive *or* cooking oil**
1/4 **teaspoon salt**
  Dash pepper
1 **7 1/2-ounce can crab meat,
    drained, flaked, and cartilage
    removed**
2 **canned green chili peppers,
    rinsed, seeded, and chopped**
1 **small avocado**
2 **cups shredded lettuce**
1 **tomato, chopped and drained**
  Lime wedges
  Bottled hot pepper sauce

In heavy skillet heat 1/4 inch oil. Fry tortillas, one at a time, in hot oil for 20 to 40 seconds on each side or till crisp and golden. Drain on paper toweling. Keep warm in foil in 250° oven.

Mix together lime juice, the 1 tablespoon oil, the salt, and pepper. Toss with crab and chili peppers. Divide mixture among tortillas. Seed, peel, and cube avocado. Top crab and peppers with lettuce, tomato, and avocado. Pass lime wedges and hot pepper sauce. Makes 8 servings.

Tostadas de Pollo *Chicken Tostadas*

8 **6-inch tortillas**
  Cooking oil
2 **whole medium chicken breasts**
1/4 **cup sliced green onion**
2 **tablespoons butter *or* margarine**
1 **8-ounce can tomato sauce**
1/2 **teaspoon garlic salt**
1/2 **teaspoon salt**
1/4 **teaspoon ground cumin**
2 **cups shredded lettuce**
1 **cup shredded monterey jack
    cheese (4 ounces)**
1 **large avocado, seeded, peeled,
    and sliced**
1/2 **cup sliced pitted ripe olives**

In small skillet cook tortillas, one at a time, in 1/4 inch hot oil for 20 to 40 seconds on each side or till crisp and golden. Drain on paper toweling; keep warm in foil in 250° oven. Skin, bone, and cut chicken breasts into very thin strips. In medium skillet quickly cook chicken and onion in butter or margarine till chicken is done and onion is tender. Add tomato sauce, garlic salt, salt, and cumin. Reduce heat and simmer, covered, for 15 to 20 minutes. To assemble each tostada, place a warm tortilla on serving plate; spoon on chicken mixture, then lettuce, cheese, avocado slices, and olives. Drizzle with bottled hot pepper sauce to taste, if desired. Makes 8 servings.

Start with a crisp flour tortilla, mound it high with colorful vegetables, then enjoy a meal-sized *Tostada Compuesta*.

Burritos *Bean and Cheese-Filled Flour Tortillas*

12 **10-inch flour tortillas**
 1 **large onion, chopped**
 2 **tablespoons cooking oil**
 4 **cups Frijoles Refritos (see page 18) *or* 2 15-ounce cans refried beans**
 1 **large tomato, chopped**
 3 **cups shredded cheddar cheese**
 1 **cup shredded lettuce**
 1 **medium avocado, seeded, peeled, and cut in 12 wedges**
 Salsa de Chile Rojo (see page 16)

Wrap stack of tortillas tightly in foil; heat in 350° oven for 15 minutes. Cook onion in oil till tender but not brown. Add Frijoles Refritos; cook and stir till heated through. Lightly salt tomato. Spoon about 1/3 cup bean mixture onto each tortilla near one edge. Top with cheese, lettuce, tomato, and avocado wedge. Fold edge nearest filling up and over filling just till mixture is covered. Fold in two sides envelope fashion, then roll up. Arrange on a baking sheet; bake in 350° oven about 15 minutes or till heated through. Pass Salsa de Chile Rojo. Makes 12.

Recipe variation: Turn these into Chimichangas by omitting the baking step and frying filled tortillas in 1/2 inch hot fat as directed in the recipe for Chimichangas, below.

Chimichangas *Fried Beef-Filled Flour Tortillas*

 2 **pounds beef stew meat**
1 1/2 **cups water**
 2 **cloves garlic, minced**
 2 **tablespoons chili powder**
 1 **tablespoon vinegar**
 2 **teaspoons dried oregano, crushed**
 1 **teaspoon salt**
 1 **teaspoon ground cumin**
 1/8 **teaspoon pepper**
 12 **10-inch flour tortillas**
 Fat for frying
 2 **cups shredded lettuce**
 2 **cups Guacamole (see page 17)**
 Radish roses

In medium saucepan combine meat, water, garlic, chili powder, vinegar, oregano, salt, cumin, and pepper. Bring to boiling. Cover; reduce heat and simmer about 2 hours or till meat is very tender. Uncover and boil rapidly about 15 minutes or until water has almost evaporated. Watch closely and stir near end of cooking time so meat doesn't stick. Remove from heat. Using 2 forks, shred meat very fine.

Meanwhile, wrap stack of tortillas in foil; heat in 350° oven for 15 minutes. Spoon about 1/4 cup meat mixture onto each tortilla, near one edge. Fold edge nearest filling up and over filling just till mixture is covered. Fold in the two sides envelope fashion, then roll up. Fasten with wooden pick, if needed.

In heavy skillet or saucepan fry filled tortillas in 1/2 inch hot fat about 1 minute on each side or till golden brown. Drain on paper toweling. Keep warm in 300° oven while frying remaining chimichangas. Garnish with lettuce, Guacamole, and radish roses. Makes 12.

Flautas de Pollo *Rolled Tortilla with Chicken Filling*

 24 **6-inch tortillas**
 3 **tablespoons butter *or* margarine**
 1/4 **cup all-purpose flour**
 1 **teaspoon salt**
 1 **cup chicken broth**
 1 **tablespoon snipped parsley**
 1 **tablespoon lemon juice**
 1 **teaspoon grated onion**
 Dash paprika
 Dash ground nutmeg
 Dash pepper
1 1/2 **cups finely diced cooked chicken**
 Fat for deep-fat frying
 Guacamole (see page 17)

Wrap tortillas tightly in foil; heat in 350° oven 20 minutes. In saucepan melt butter or margarine; blend in flour and salt. Add chicken broth. Cook and stir till mixture thickens. Add parsley, lemon juice, onion, paprika, nutmeg, and pepper. Stir in chicken; cool slightly. Place about 1 tablespoon chicken mixture on each tortilla. Roll up very tightly, securing with wooden picks. Fry in deep hot fat (350°) for 1 to 2 minutes. Garnish with Guacamole. Makes 4 to 6 servings.

Papatzul Egg-Stuffed Tortillas in Pumpkin Seed Sauce

1 cup shelled pumpkin seeds
  (4 ounces)
1 4-ounce can green chili
  peppers, rinsed, seeded,
  and finely chopped
1/2 teaspoon dried epazote,
  crushed (optional)
1/4 teaspoon salt
1 1/2 cups water
12 6-inch corn tortillas
1 16-ounce can tomatoes
1 medium onion, cut up
2 teaspoons cornstarch
1 teaspoon salt
1/4 teaspoon sugar
1/8 teaspoon pepper
2 tablespoons cooking oil
6 hard-cooked eggs, chopped

Toast pumpkin seeds in 350° oven for 15 minutes. Place pumpkin seeds in blender container; cover and blend till coarsely chopped. Turn into saucepan; add chopped chili peppers, *half* the epazote, and the 1/4 teaspoon salt. Slowly add water. Cook and stir over low heat for 20 minutes; do not boil. Cover and keep warm.

Meanwhile, wrap stack of tortillas tightly in foil; heat about 15 minutes in 350° oven. In same blender container combine *undrained* tomatoes, onion, cornstarch, the 1 teaspoon salt, sugar, pepper, and remaining epazote. Cover and blend till smooth. Pour into saucepan; add oil. Cook and stir till thickened and bubbly.

Season eggs lightly with salt and pepper. Spread about 2 teaspoons of the pumpkin seed mixture on each tortilla. Top each with about 2 tablespoons chopped egg. Roll up. Place seam side down in a 13x9x2-inch baking dish. Pour remaining pumpkin seed sauce over tortillas; top with tomato sauce mixture. Bake, covered, in 350° oven for 20 to 25 minutes or till hot. Makes 12 servings.

About this recipe: Like many tasty recipes from Yucatan, Papatzul features epazote among its seasonings. Although there is no substitute for this herb, you may omit it and still achieve delicious results (see page 9).

Panuchos Black Bean-Stuffed Tortillas

1/2 pound black beans (1 1/4 cups)
3 cups water
2 whole medium chicken breasts
  (1 1/2 pounds)
1 cup water
1/2 teaspoon salt
12 6-inch tortillas
  Fat for deep-fat frying
1/2 cup chopped onion
1/2 cup lard *or* bacon drippings
1 4-ounce can green chili
  peppers, rinsed, seeded, and
  chopped
1 teaspoon salt
2 hard-cooked eggs, each cut in 6
  slices
2 medium onions, thinly sliced
1/2 cup vinegar
6 whole peppercorns
3 cloves garlic, minced
1 bay leaf
1/4 teaspoon dried oregano,
  crushed
1/4 teaspoon cumin seed
  Salsa Cruda (see page 17)

In large saucepan soak black beans overnight in the 3 cups water. (Or, bring to boiling; simmer 2 minutes. Cover and let stand 1 hour.) Do not drain. Simmer beans about 1 1/2 hours or till very tender.

In medium saucepan place chicken breasts, the 1 cup water, and 1/2 teaspoon salt. Bring to boiling; reduce heat and simmer about 20 minutes or till tender. Drain, reserving broth. Skin and bone chicken; shred meat and set aside.

Holding a tortilla with tongs, slip it into deep hot fat (375°) and fry for 5 to 10 seconds or till tortilla puffs. Turn and fry second side 10 seconds more or till browned. Drain on paper toweling. Repeat with remaining tortillas.

In large skillet cook chopped onion in lard about 5 minutes or till tender. Add beans with liquid, chili peppers, and 1 teaspoon salt. Mash beans in skillet. Cook, uncovered, over medium heat 5 minutes or till very thick.

Carefully make a slit at base of puff in each tortilla. Fill tortillas with about 2 tablespoons beans and 1 slice egg. Arrange on baking sheet and bake 10 minutes in 350° oven.

In saucepan combine onions, vinegar, peppercorns, garlic, bay leaf, oregano, cumin, and 1/2 cup reserved chicken broth. Simmer, covered, for 5 minutes. Remove bay leaf. Add chicken; heat through. Drain. Spoon chicken and onions over hot panuchos. Pass Salsa Cruda. Serves 6.

About this recipe: Some canned and frozen tortillas are difficult to make puff. If you have trouble, you can layer foods on top as for a tostada.

Enchiladas Rojas   Red Enchiladas (photo on page 19)

2 dried ancho chilies *or* 1/2
  teaspoon crushed red pepper
1 8-ounce can tomatoes
1 small onion, cut up
1 clove garlic
1/2 teaspoon salt
1 tablespoon cooking oil
1/2 cup whipping cream
  Salt and pepper
1 pound chorizo *or* Italian
  sausage
2 tablespoons cooking oil
12 6-inch tortillas
1/2 cup shredded cheddar cheese
  (2 ounces)
1/4 cup sliced green onion

Remove stems and seeds from chilies; cut up. Place in bowl; cover with boiling water. Let stand 45 to 60 minutes; drain. In blender container combine *undrained* tomatoes, onion, garlic, salt, and the drained chilies or crushed red pepper. Blend till smooth. In medium saucepan combine blended mixture and the 1 tablespoon oil. Cook and stir about 3 minutes or till slightly thickened. Stir in whipping cream; season to taste with salt and pepper.

Chop chorizo or sausage; brown in skillet. Drain off fat. Combine sausage with 2/3 *cup* of the sauce. In small skillet heat 2 tablespoons oil. Dip each tortilla in the hot oil for about 10 seconds or just till limp. Drain on paper toweling. Spoon filling onto tortillas; roll up. Arrange filled tortillas in a 13x9x2-inch baking dish. Pour remaining sauce down center of tortillas. Bake, covered, in 350° oven for 20 minutes or till heated through. Sprinkle with cheese; bake, uncovered, 1 or 2 minutes longer or till cheese melts. Just before serving sprinkle with green onion. Makes 6 servings.

Chilaquiles   Tortilla Skillet (photo on page 51)

6 6-inch tortillas
  Cooking oil
4 slightly beaten eggs
1/4 teaspoon salt
2 1/4 cups Salsa de Chile Rojo (see
  page 16)
1 1/2 cups crumbled soft Mexican *or*
  farmer cheese (6 ounces)
1/2 cup water
1/4 cup sliced green onion

Tear tortillas in 1 1/2-inch pieces. Heat 1/2 inch oil in heavy saucepan or deep skillet. Fry tortilla pieces in hot oil for 45 to 60 seconds or till crisp and golden. Remove with slotted spoon; drain on paper toweling. Pour all but 2 tablespoons oil from skillet; return tortillas to skillet. Stir in eggs and salt; cook and stir till tortillas are coated and eggs are set. Stir in Salsa de Chile Rojo, *1 cup* of the cheese, the water, and *half* the onion. Simmer, uncovered, for 15 minutes. Turn into serving dish; top with remaining cheese and onion. Makes 4 servings.

Enchiladas de Pollo y Queso   Chicken Enchilada Casserole

1 cup chopped onion
1/2 cup chopped green bell pepper
2 tablespoons butter *or* margarine
2 cups chopped cooked chicken
  or turkey
1 4-ounce can green chili
  peppers, rinsed, seeded, and
  chopped
3 tablespoons butter *or* margarine
1/4 cup all-purpose flour
1 teaspoon ground coriander
  seed
3/4 teaspoon salt
2 1/2 cups chicken broth
1 cup dairy sour cream
1 1/2 cups shredded monterey jack
  cheese (6 ounces)
12 6-inch tortillas

In large saucepan cook onion and green pepper in the 2 tablespoons butter or margarine till tender. Combine in a bowl with chopped chicken and green chili peppers; set aside.

In same saucepan melt the 3 tablespoons butter or margarine. Blend in flour, coriander, and salt. Stir in chicken broth all at once; cook and stir till thickened and bubbly. Remove from heat; stir in sour cream and 1/2 *cup* of cheese. Stir 1/2 *cup* of the sauce into the chicken. Dip each tortilla into remaining hot sauce to soften; fill each with about 1/4 *cup* of the chicken mixture. Roll up. Arrange rolls in a 13x9x2-inch baking dish; pour remaining sauce over. Sprinkle with remaining cheese. Bake, uncovered, in 350° oven about 25 minutes or till bubbly. Serves 6.

Enchiladas Verdes Hot Pepper Enchiladas

2 tablespoons cooking oil
12 6-inch tortillas
2 cups shredded monterey jack cheese (8 ounces)
¾ cup chopped onion
¼ cup butter *or* margarine
¼ cup all-purpose flour
2 cups chicken broth
1 4-ounce can pickled jalapeño peppers, rinsed, seeded, and chopped
1 cup dairy sour cream
1 medium tomato, finely chopped
½ cup finely chopped onion
¼ cup tomato juice
½ teaspoon salt

In small skillet heat oil. Dip each tortilla in hot oil for 10 seconds or just till limp. Drain on paper toweling.

Place *2 tablespoons* of the shredded cheese and *1 tablespoon* onion on each tortilla; roll up. Place tortillas, seam side down, in 12x7½x2-inch baking dish.

In medium saucepan melt butter or margarine; blend in flour. Add chicken broth all at once; cook, stirring constantly, till thickened and bubbly. Reserve 1 tablespoon chopped peppers. Stir sour cream and remaining peppers into sauce; cook till heated through *but do not boil*. Pour sauce over rolled tortillas in baking dish. Bake in 425° oven for 20 minutes. Sprinkle remaining ½ cup shredded cheese atop tortillas; return to oven for about 5 minutes or just till cheese melts.

In bowl combine tomato, the ½ cup onion, tomato juice, salt, and the 1 tablespoon reserved chopped peppers. Pass with enchiladas. Makes 6 servings.

Enchiladas de Pollo Chicken Enchiladas

1 16-ounce can tomatoes
1 4-ounce can green chili peppers, rinsed and seeded
½ teaspoon coriander seed
½ teaspoon salt
1 cup dairy sour cream
2 cups finely chopped cooked chicken *or* turkey
1 3-ounce package cream cheese, softened
¼ cup finely chopped onion
¾ teaspoon salt
2 tablespoons cooking oil
12 6-inch tortillas
1 cup shredded monterey jack cheese (4 ounces)

Place *undrained* tomatoes, chili peppers, coriander seed, and the ½ teaspoon salt in blender container. Cover; blend till mixture is smooth. Add sour cream; cover and blend just till combined. Set aside.

Combine chicken or turkey, cream cheese, onion, and ¾ teaspoon salt. In skillet heat cooking oil. Dip tortillas, one at a time, into hot oil for 10 seconds or just till limp. Drain on paper toweling. Spoon chicken mixture on tortillas; roll up. Place seam side down in 12x7½x2-inch baking dish. Pour tomato mixture atop. Cover with foil; bake in 350° oven about 30 minutes or till heated through. Remove foil; sprinkle with shredded cheese. Return to oven till cheese melts. Makes 6 servings.

Enchiladas Empalmadas Stacked Enchiladas

½ cup finely chopped onion
2 tablespoons cooking oil
1 tablespoon all-purpose flour
½ cup milk
1 4-ounce can green chili peppers, rinsed, seeded, and chopped
½ teaspoon salt
2 cups diced cooked beef
2 tomatoes, peeled and chopped
2 tablespoons cooking oil
8 6-inch tortillas
1 cup shredded monterey jack cheese (4 ounces)

In skillet cook onion in 2 tablespoons oil till tender but not brown. Blend in flour. Add milk, chili peppers, and salt. Cook, stirring constantly, till thickened and bubbly. Stir in beef and tomatoes. Heat through; keep warm.

In small skillet heat 2 tablespoons oil. Holding tortilla with tongs, dip in hot oil for 10 seconds or till limp. Drain on paper toweling. Place a hot tortilla in 9x9x2-inch baking pan. Top with about ¼ cup beef mixture and 2 tablespoons of cheese. Layer on remaining tortillas, beef mixture, and cheese to make a stack. Bake in 350° oven for 20 minutes or till hot. Unstack to serve. Serves 4.

Carnes Meats

Albóndigas Meatballs

1 beaten egg
¾ cup soft bread crumbs (1 slice)
¼ cup milk
½ teaspoon salt
¼ teaspoon pepper
¼ teaspoon dried oregano, crushed
1 pound ground beef
½ pound ground pork
24 pimiento-stuffed olives
1 16-ounce can tomatoes, cut up
½ cup water
¼ cup finely chopped onion
2 teaspoons instant beef bouillon granules
1 clove garlic, minced
¼ teaspoon dried oregano, crushed
Several dashes bottled hot pepper sauce

In bowl combine egg, bread crumbs, milk, salt, pepper, and ¼ teaspoon oregano; mix well. Add beef and pork; combine thoroughly. Shape meat mixture into 24 meatballs around the 24 olives. Set aside.

In 10-inch skillet combine *undrained* tomatoes, water, onion, bouillon granules, garlic, ¼ teaspoon oregano, and bottled hot pepper sauce. Bring to boiling; simmer, uncovered, for 15 minutes. Drop meatballs into sauce; cover and simmer about 30 minutes or till meatballs are done. Remove meatballs from sauce; cover and keep warm. Skim excess fat from sauce. Boil sauce about 10 minutes to reduce mixture to 1½ cups. Serve over meatballs. Makes 6 servings.

Mole de Olla Beef Stew in a Pot

2 pounds beef stew meat, cut in 1-inch pieces
2 tablespoons cooking oil
3 cups water
¼ cup snipped parsley
2 teaspoons salt
⅛ teaspoon pepper
2 dried ancho chilies*
2 dried pasilla chilies*
1 16-ounce can tomatoes
1 medium onion, cut up
½ cup water
2 tablespoons sesame seed
2 cloves garlic
1 teaspoon instant beef bouillon granules
⅛ teaspoon ground cumin
2 medium zucchini *or* summer squash, cut up (1 pound)
3 small potatoes, peeled and quartered
2 ears fresh corn, cut in 1-inch pieces
* *Or* substitute 1 teaspoon crushed red pepper for the dried ancho and pasilla chilies

In Dutch oven brown meat, half at a time, in hot oil. Return all meat to Dutch oven. Add the 3 cups water, parsley, salt, and pepper. Cover; simmer 1½ hours.

Cut ancho and pasilla chilies open. Discard stems and seeds. Cut chilies into small pieces with scissors or a knife. Place in a bowl; cover with boiling water and let stand 45 to 60 minutes. Drain.

In blender container place *undrained* tomatoes, drained chilies or crushed red pepper, onion, the ½ cup water, sesame seed, garlic, bouillon granules, and cumin; blend till nearly smooth. Add to beef mixture along with squash, potatoes, and corn. Cover and simmer 25 to 30 minutes or till meat is tender and vegetables are done. Season to taste with salt and pepper. Makes 8 to 10 servings.

Mole de Olla, a beef stew with fresh corn and zucchini, owes its name to the earthenware pot or *olla* used to cook it.

Pozole Hominy Stew

1½ pounds beef stew meat, cut in
   ½-inch pieces
4 cups water
½ cup chopped onion
1½ teaspoons salt
2 15-ounce cans hominy, drained
1 10-ounce can tomatoes with
   green chilies
½ cup cold water
¼ cup all-purpose flour
   Shredded cabbage
   Sliced green onion
   Sliced radish

In 3-quart saucepan combine beef, the 4 cups water, onion, and salt. Cover; simmer 1½ hours. Add hominy and *undrained* tomatoes with chilies. Cover; simmer 30 minutes more. Blend the ½ cup cold water into flour; add to beef mixture. Cook and stir till thickened and bubbly. Serve in bowls; top with cabbage, green onion, and radish. Makes 6 to 8 servings.

Ropa Vieja Shredded Beef

1 pound cooked beef pot roast *or*
   brisket
½ cup water
2 tablespoons finely chopped
   onion
2 tablespoons finely chopped red
   or green bell pepper
1 teaspoon instant beef bouillon
   granules
1 tablespoon cooking oil
2 cups finely diced cooked potato
   (2 medium)
1 hard-cooked egg, sliced
1 tablespoon snipped parsley

In covered skillet heat meat with water, onion, chopped pepper, and bouillon for about 30 minutes or till most of the liquid is absorbed and meat will shred easily.

Remove skillet from heat. Using two forks, pull meat apart into shreds. Return to heat. Push meat mixture to one side of skillet. In open area of skillet heat oil; add potatoes. Cook and stir meat and potatoes together in oil till mixture is heated through and almost dry. Season to taste with salt and pepper.

Transfer meat mixture to serving platter. Garnish with egg slices. Sprinkle with parsley. Makes 4 to 6 servings.

About this recipe: The delicious flavor of this dish belies the literal translation of its name—"old clothes." *Ropa Vieja* is also a tasty filling for tacos or burritos.

Chile con Carne Hot Chili with Meat

5 slices bacon
8 ounces chorizo *or* Italian
   sausage links, sliced
1½ pounds beef stew meat, diced
2 medium onions, chopped (1 cup)
1 small green bell pepper,
   chopped
1 clove garlic, minced
2 pickled jalapeño peppers,
   rinsed, seeded, and chopped
1 to 1½ tablespoons chili powder
½ teaspoon crushed red pepper
½ teaspoon salt
¼ teaspoon dried oregano,
   crushed
2½ cups water
1 12-ounce can tomato paste
1 15½-ounce can pinto beans,
   drained

In large saucepan or Dutch oven cook bacon till crisp; drain and crumble. Discard drippings; set bacon aside. Brown sausage in same pan. Drain sausage, reserving 2 tablespoons drippings; set sausage aside. In reserved drippings brown diced beef, onions, green pepper, and garlic. Add the cooked bacon, sausage, jalapeño peppers, chili powder, crushed red pepper, salt, and oregano. Stir in water and tomato paste. Bring to boiling; simmer, uncovered, for 1½ hours, stirring occasionally. Stir in beans; simmer, covered, 30 minutes more. Makes 8 servings.

A radish-topped hominy and beef stew called *Pozole* is flanked by *Chilaquiles* (see page 46) and two popular table sauces, *Salsa de Chile Rojo* (see page 16) and *Guacamole* (see page 17).

Carne Claveteada *Studded Pot Roast*

1 **3-pound beef brisket**
5 **slices bacon, cut up**
2 **tablespoons slivered almonds**
2 **tablespoons cooking oil**
³/₄ **cup water**
1 **4-ounce can green chili peppers, rinsed, seeded, and chopped**
2 **tablespoons vinegar**
2 **cloves garlic, minced**
1 **teaspoon salt**
¹/₄ **teaspoon ground cinnamon**
¹/₄ **teaspoon dried thyme, crushed**
¹/₄ **teaspoon dried marjoram, crushed**
¹/₄ **teaspoon dried oregano, crushed**
¹/₈ **teaspoon ground cloves**
¹/₈ **teaspoon pepper**
4 **large potatoes, peeled and cut into pieces**

Trim visible fat from brisket. Cut small slits about 1 inch deep in top surface of meat and stud with raw bacon pieces and slivered almonds. In a large Dutch oven brown studded brisket on both sides in hot cooking oil.

Combine water, chopped chili peppers, vinegar, garlic, salt, cinnamon, thyme, marjoram, oregano, cloves, and pepper. Pour chili mixture over meat. Cover; simmer for 1 hour and 45 minutes. Add potatoes and, if needed, more water. Cover; simmer 45 minutes more or till potatoes are tender. Makes 6 servings.

Mochomos Shredded Pork Chihuahua-Style

2 **pounds boneless pork shoulder,**
   cut in 1-inch pieces
2 **cups water**
1 **small onion, quartered**
1 **teaspoon salt**
2 **cups Guacamole (see page 17)**
   Tomato slices
   Shredded lettuce

In saucepan bring meat, water, onion, and salt to boiling. Simmer, covered, for 1 hour till meat is very tender. Uncover; boil rapidly 15 to 20 minutes or till most of water evaporates. Watch closely and stir near end of time so meat doesn't stick and burn. Using 2 forks, finely shred meat. In lightly greased skillet fry meat till it resembles golden threads. Mound on platter; spoon Guacamole around edge. Garnish with tomato and lettuce. Serves 6 to 8.

Chiles en Nogada Chilies in Nut Sauce (photo on page 39)

1 **pound ground pork**
1 **small onion, chopped**
1 **clove garlic, minced**
1 **8 ³/₄-ounce can sliced peaches,**
   drained
1 **medium pear, peeled and cored**
1 **8-ounce can tomato sauce**
¹/₄ **cup raisins**
³/₄ **teaspoon salt**
¹/₄ **teaspoon ground cinnamon**
6 **large green bell peppers** *or*
   poblano chilies
   Nut Sauce
¹/₄ **cup pomegranate seeds**
   (optional)

In skillet cook pork, onion, and garlic till meat is brown and onion is tender. Drain off fat. Chop peaches and pear; add to meat along with tomato sauce, raisins, salt, and cinnamon. Simmer, uncovered, for 10 minutes.

Meanwhile, cut tops from peppers; remove seeds and veins. Cook in large amount boiling salted water for about 10 minutes or till crisp-tender; drain. Sprinkle insides of peppers with salt. Spoon meat filling into peppers; place in shallow baking dish. Bake in 350° oven for 20 minutes or till heated through. To serve, top peppers with Nut Sauce; sprinkle with pomegranate seeds. Makes 6 servings.

Nut Sauce: In blender or with mortar and pestle, grind ¹/₄ cup *walnuts* and ¹/₄ cup blanched *almonds*. Combine 1 cup dairy *sour cream* and ¹/₄ cup *milk*. Stir in the nuts, ¹/₈ teaspoon ground *cinnamon*, dash *salt,* and dash *pepper.*

Mancha Manteles de Cerdo Pork Stew with Fruit (photo on page 38)

2 **dried ancho chilies***
2 **dried pasilla chilies***
2 **pounds boneless pork**
2 **cups water**
1 **bay leaf**
¹/₂ **teaspoon dried thyme, crushed**
¹/₂ **teaspoon dried oregano, crushed**
2 **whole cloves**
1 **12-ounce can tomatillos**
1 **small onion, cut up**
4 **sprigs cilantro** *or* **parsley**
1 **clove garlic, cut up**
2 **tart cooking apples**
2 **firm pears**
2 **small zucchini, sliced**
1 **10-ounce package frozen peas**
1 **8¹/₄-ounce can pineapple**
   chunks, drained
2 **green-tipped bananas, sliced**
¹/₄ **cup chopped walnuts**
 * *Or* **substitute 1 teaspoon crushed**
   red pepper for the dried ancho
   and pasilla chilies

Cut chilies open. Discard stems and seeds. Cut chilies into small pieces with scissors or a knife. Place in bowl; cover with boiling water. Let stand 45 to 60 minutes; drain.

Cut pork in 1-inch cubes. In Dutch oven combine pork, water, bay leaf, thyme, oregano, cloves, 1 teaspoon *salt,* and ¹/₈ teaspoon *pepper.* Cover and simmer 40 minutes or till pork is nearly tender. Drain pork, reserving 2 cups broth. Rinse, drain, and halve tomatillos. In blender container combine the tomatillos, onion, the drained peppers or crushed red pepper, cilantro, garlic, and reserved broth. Cover and blend till smooth.

Peel, core, and slice apples and pears; add to pork along with tomatillo mixture and zucchini. Cover and simmer 10 minutes. Add peas, pineapple, bananas, and walnuts; simmer 5 minutes more. Makes 8 servings.

About this recipe: Although the title means "pork tablecloth-stainer," this flavor-packed stew translates into a delectable main dish.

Chuletas de Puerco Adobadas *Pork Chops in Adobo Sauce*

1 8-ounce can tomato sauce
¼ cup vinegar
1 medium onion, cut up
2 cloves garlic
2 tablespoons all-purpose flour
2 tablespoons chili powder
1 tablespoon cooking oil
1 teaspoon salt
½ teaspoon dried oregano, crushed
¼ teaspoon cumin seed
6 pork loin chops, cut ½-inch thick
Sliced onion
Sliced radish
Sliced avocado

Place tomato sauce, vinegar, onion, garlic, flour, chili powder, oil, salt, oregano, and cumin in blender container. Cover; blend till onion is finely chopped. Place chops in shallow baking dish. Pour sauce over. Cover; refrigerate several hours or overnight.

In large covered skillet, simmer chops in sauce 35 to 45 minutes or till tender. Arrange chops with sauce on a serving platter. Garnish with sliced onion, radish, and avocado. Makes 6 servings.

Pierna de Carnero *Marinated Leg of Lamb*

1 4½- to 5-pound leg of lamb, with shank bone cut short
3 cloves garlic, cut up
1 cup white wine vinegar
½ cup olive oil *or* cooking oil
½ cup chopped onion
½ cup chopped carrot
1 small turnip, peeled and chopped
¼ cup snipped parsley
1 teaspoon sugar
1 teaspoon salt
½ teaspoon dried oregano, crushed
⅛ teaspoon pepper

With sharp knife make 8 or 9 slits in the meat. Insert a piece of garlic in each slit. Prick meat at about 1½-inch intervals. Place meat in large plastic bag or in a shallow baking dish. Combine remaining ingredients; pour over meat. Close plastic bag if used; lay in shallow baking pan. Marinate in refrigerator at least 24 hours, turning occasionally.

Remove meat from bag or dish, reserving marinade. Place meat, fat side up, on a rack in a shallow roasting pan; do not add water. Insert meat thermometer into thickest part of muscle, making sure it doesn't touch bone. Roast in 325° oven for 2 to 3 hours or till thermometer reaches 170° to 180°. Let stand 15 minutes before carving.

In saucepan bring reserved marinade to a boil. Cover and simmer 10 to 15 minutes or till vegetables are tender. Spoon over meat. Makes 10 to 12 servings.

Ternera en Nogada *Veal in Pecan Sauce*

1½ pounds boneless veal, cut in 1-inch pieces
½ cup water
¼ cup chopped onion
1 teaspoon instant chicken bouillon granules
1 clove garlic, minced
½ teaspoon salt
¼ teaspoon dried thyme, crushed
¼ teaspoon dried oregano, crushed
¼ cup chopped onion
¼ cup chopped pecans
1 tablespoon butter *or* margarine
3 tablespoons all-purpose flour
½ cup dairy sour cream

In 3-quart saucepan combine veal, water, ¼ cup onion, bouillon granules, garlic, salt, thyme, and oregano. Simmer, covered, about 45 to 60 minutes or till meat is tender. Drain meat, reserving broth. Measure broth and add water, if needed, to make 1½ cups.

In small saucepan cook ¼ cup onion and chopped pecans in butter or margarine till onion is tender but not brown. Remove saucepan from heat. Blend flour into sour cream; stir in reserved broth mixture. Add to veal along with pecan mixture; mix well. Return to heat. Cook and stir till sauce is thickened and meat is heated through. Serve with hot cooked rice, if desired. Makes 6 servings.

Pollo Aguascalientes Chicken Aguascalientes-Style

1 2½- to 3-pound broiler-fryer
  chicken, cut up
2 tablespoons cooking oil
1 small onion, thinly sliced
1 clove garlic, minced
3 medium tomatoes, peeled,
  seeded, and chopped
1 tablespoon lemon juice
1 teaspoon sugar
1 teaspoon salt
1 teaspoon dried oregano,
  crushed
⅛ teaspoon ground cinnamon
⅛ teaspoon ground cloves
2 teaspoons cornstarch

Sprinkle chicken with salt and pepper. In 12-inch skillet brown chicken in cooking oil about 15 minutes. Add onion and garlic; cook 5 minutes more. Add tomatoes, lemon juice, sugar, salt, oregano, cinnamon, cloves, and ½ cup *water*. Cover; simmer 30 to 35 minutes or till chicken is tender. Remove chicken to platter, keep warm. Measure pan juices; add water to make 2 cups. Return to skillet. Combine cornstarch and 2 tablespoons *cold water;* add to skillet. Cook and stir till thickened and bubbly. Spoon some sauce over chicken; pass remainder. Garnish platter with shredded lettuce and jalapeño peppers, if desired. Makes 4 servings.

About this recipe: Aguascalientes, located northwest of Mexico City, is the home of this flavorful chicken, traditionally served with fried potatoes, peppers, and chorizo.

Pollo en Vino Rojo Chicken in Red Wine

1 2½- to 3-pound broiler-fryer
  chicken, cut up
½ cup vinegar
¼ cup olive oil *or* cooking oil
1 small onion, chopped
1 clove garlic
1 bay leaf
½ teaspoon dried oregano, crushed
½ teaspoon salt
2 slices bacon, cut up
1 8-ounce can tomatoes, cut up
1 carrot, chopped (½ cup)
1 cup dry red wine

Place chicken pieces in plastic bag in deep bowl. Combine vinegar, oil, onion, garlic, bay leaf, oregano, salt, and ⅛ teaspoon *pepper*. Pour over chicken; close bag and marinate 6 to 8 hours in refrigerator.

In 12-inch skillet cook bacon till crisp; drain, reserving drippings. Crumble bacon and set aside. Drain chicken, reserving marinade. Brown chicken pieces in reserved drippings, about 15 minutes. Drain off fat. Remove garlic and bay leaf from marinade. Pour marinade over chicken in skillet. Add *undrained* tomatoes, carrot, and wine. Cover and cook over low heat 35 to 40 minutes or till chicken is tender. Remove chicken. Stir bacon into sauce; season with salt and pepper. Spoon over chicken. Serves 4.

Pato en Jugo de Naranja Duck in Orange Juice

1 4- to 5-pound frozen duckling,
  thawed and quartered
2 tablespoons cooking oil
1 cup orange juice
2 tomatoes, peeled, seeded, and
  chopped
½ cup finely chopped onion
1 clove garlic, minced
¼ cup toasted slivered almonds
¼ cup raisins
¼ cup snipped parsley
1 bay leaf
¼ teaspoon dried thyme, crushed
⅛ teaspoon dried oregano, crushed
¼ cup dry sherry
2 tablespoons all-purpose flour

Sprinkle duckling with salt and pepper. In 12-inch skillet brown duckling pieces slowly on both sides in hot oil; drain off fat. Add orange juice, tomatoes, onion, garlic, almonds, raisins, parsley, bay leaf, thyme, oregano, and ½ teaspoon *salt*. Cover and simmer 45 to 50 minutes or till duckling is tender. Remove to serving plate; keep warm. Skim excess fat from pan juices; measure juices. Add water, if necessary, to make 1¼ cups; return to skillet. Stir sherry into flour; stir into skillet mixture. Cook and stir till thickened and bubbly. Season to taste with salt and pepper. Spoon over duckling. Makes 4 servings.

Serve *Pollo Aguascalientes* with jalapeño peppers to provide desired hotness, and fried potatoes.

Pollo Almendrado Rojo Red Chicken with Almonds

1/4 cup all-purpose flour
2 teaspoons salt
1/2 teaspoon dried thyme, crushed
1/4 teaspoon pepper
1 2 1/2- to 3-pound broiler-fryer
    chicken, cut up
2 tablespoons cooking oil
1 large onion, finely chopped
2 teaspoons paprika
1 clove garlic, minced
1 8-ounce can tomatoes, cut up
1/2 cup water
1/2 cup toasted blanched almonds

In plastic or paper bag combine flour, *1 teaspoon* of the salt, the thyme, and pepper. Add chicken pieces a few at a time; shake to coat. In 12-inch skillet brown chicken pieces in hot oil about 15 minutes. Add onion, paprika, and garlic; cook 5 minutes longer. Stir in *undrained* tomatoes, water, and remaining 1 teaspoon salt. Place toasted almonds in blender container; cover and blend till almonds are finely chopped. Add to chicken. Cover and simmer 30 to 35 minutes or till chicken is tender. Makes 4 servings.

Arroz con Pollo Chicken with Rice

1 2 1/2- to 3-pound broiler-fryer
    chicken, cut up
2 tablespoons cooking oil
1 1/2 cups long grain rice
1 cup chopped onion
2 cloves garlic, minced
3 cups water
1 8-ounce can tomatoes, cut up
1 tablespoon instant chicken
    bouillon granules
1 teaspoon salt
1/4 teaspoon pepper
1/4 teaspoon saffron, crushed
1 cup frozen peas
1 2-ounce can sliced pimiento,
    drained and chopped

Sprinkle chicken lightly with salt. In 12-inch skillet brown chicken in hot oil about 15 minutes. Remove chicken from pan. In drippings remaining in pan, cook rice, onion, and garlic till rice is golden. Add water, *undrained* tomatoes, bouillon granules, salt, pepper, and saffron. Bring to boiling; stir well. Arrange chicken atop rice mixture. Cover and simmer 30 to 35 minutes or till chicken is tender. Add peas and chopped pimiento; cover and cook 5 minutes more. Makes 4 to 6 servings.

Pollo Tapado Chicken Stew with Bananas

1 2 1/2- to 3-pound broiler-fryer
    chicken, cut up
2 tablespoons cooking oil
1 small onion, sliced
1 pound summer squash *or*
    zucchini, cut in 1/2-inch slices
    (about 4 cups)
2 slices fresh pineapple, cut 1/2
    inch thick *or* 1 8-ounce can
    pineapple slices (juice pack)
2 tablespoons brown sugar
1 tablespoon instant chicken
    bouillon granules
1 8-ounce can tomatoes, cut up
2 firm pears
1 green-tipped banana, unpeeled
1 cup frozen peas

In 4-quart Dutch oven brown chicken well in hot oil, about 15 minutes. Drain off fat. Sprinkle chicken with salt. Place onion, squash, and pineapple atop chicken (include juice if canned pineapple is used). Stir brown sugar and bouillon granules into *undrained* tomatoes; pour over chicken. Cover; simmer 25 minutes. Peel, core, and slice pears into mixture. Without peeling banana, cut crosswise into 8 pieces. Add to mixture along with peas. Cover and simmer 15 minutes longer. Remove banana peel. Serve in bowls. Makes 4 servings.

About this recipe: Although *tapado* in the title refers specifically to bananas, the combination of several fruits and vegetables gives this colorful dish flavor as well as eye appeal. Incidentally, leaving the peel on the banana slices until serving time helps to hold their shape during cooking.

Guajolote Relleno *Stuffed Turkey*

1 pound finely ground *or*
　twice-ground pork
1/2 cup chopped onion
1 clove garlic, minced
2 tomatoes, peeled, seeded, and
　chopped
1 small green-tipped banana,
　peeled and chopped
1 tart apple, peeled, cored, and
　chopped
1/4 cup raisins
2 tablespoons toasted slivered
　almonds
1 pickled jalapeño pepper, rinsed,
　seeded, and chopped
1 1/2 teaspoons salt
1 8- to 10-pound turkey
1/4 cup butter *or* margarine, melted
　Chicken broth
1/2 cup dry white wine
1/4 cup all-purpose flour

In large skillet cook pork, onion, and garlic till meat is brown and onion is tender, stirring to break up any lumps. Drain off excess fat. Stir in tomatoes, banana, apple, raisins, almonds, chopped jalapeño pepper, and salt. Cook and stir for two minutes. Remove from heat; add salt and pepper to taste. Cool slightly.

To stuff turkey, loosely spoon some of the stuffing into the neck cavity; pull the neck skin to the back of bird and fasten securely with a small skewer. Lightly spoon remaining stuffing into the body cavity. If opening has a band of skin across the tail, tuck drumsticks under band; if not, tie legs securely to tail. Twist wing tips under back.

Place bird, breast side up, on a rack in a shallow roasting pan. Brush with the melted butter or margarine. Cover bird loosely with foil. Roast in 325° oven for 4 to 4 1/2 hours or till done, brushing occasionally with butter. After 3 hours, cut band of skin or string between legs so thighs will cook evenly. Remove foil during last 45 minutes of cooking time. Remove turkey to platter. Let stand 15 minutes before carving.

Meanwhile, spoon excess fat from pan drippings; add chicken broth to remaining drippings to equal 2 cups. Return to pan. Stir wine into flour; stir into pan drippings. Cook and stir till thickened and bubbly. Pass with turkey. Makes 8 to 12 servings.

Pollo Borracho *Drunken Chicken (photo on page 39)*

1/4 cup chopped onion
1 clove garlic, minced
1/2 teaspoon chili powder
1 tablespoon cooking oil
1 8-ounce can tomato sauce
1/4 cup rum *or* sherry
1/4 cup water
1/4 cup diced fully cooked ham
2 tablespoons raisins
2 tablespoons sliced
　pimiento-stuffed olives
1 bay leaf
2 teaspoons capers
1/2 teaspoon salt
1/4 teaspoon dried oregano,
　crushed
1/8 teaspoon dried thyme, crushed
1/8 teaspoon dried marjoram,
　crushed
　Dash pepper
1 2 1/2- to 3-pound broiler-fryer
　chicken, cut up
2 tablespoons water
4 teaspoons cornstarch
1 hard-cooked egg, chopped

In 4 1/2-quart Dutch oven cook onion, garlic, and chili powder in oil till onion is tender but not brown. Stir in tomato sauce, rum or sherry, the 1/4 cup water, diced ham, raisins, olives, bay leaf, capers, salt, oregano, thyme, marjoram, and pepper. Add chicken pieces to Dutch oven, turning to coat. Cover and bake in 350° oven for 1 hour. Uncover and bake 15 minutes more.

Transfer chicken to serving platter; cover and keep warm. Remove bay leaf. Skim fat from pan. Measure juices; add water if needed to make 1 1/2 cups. Return to Dutch oven. Stir the 2 tablespoons water into cornstarch. Add to juices. On range top cook and stir till thickened and bubbly. Spoon atop chicken. Garnish chicken with chopped hard-cooked egg. Makes 3 or 4 servings.

Peanut butter lends its name and flavor to *Pollo en Mole de Cacahuate,* Chicken with Peanut Mole Sauce. Bake it in a favorite casserole or in a colorful Mexican pottery *cazuela.*

Pollo en Mole Verde *Chicken in Green Mole Sauce*

- **¹/₃ cup all-purpose flour**
- **1 teaspoon paprika**
- **1 teaspoon salt**
- **¹/₄ teaspoon pepper**
- **1 2¹/₂- to 3-pound broiler-fryer chicken, cut up**
- **2 tablespoons cooking oil**
- **1 12-ounce can tomatillos, drained and rinsed**
- **1 4-ounce can green chili peppers, rinsed, seeded, and cut up**
- **¹/₄ cup chicken broth**
- **1 small onion, cut up**
- **¹/₄ cup chopped walnuts**
- **¹/₄ cup blanched almonds**
- **Several sprigs cilantro**
- **¹/₄ teaspoon salt**
- **Dash pepper**

In a paper or plastic bag combine flour, paprika, the 1 teaspoon salt, and the ¹/₄ teaspoon pepper. Add 2 or 3 pieces of chicken at a time; shake to coat. In a large skillet brown chicken pieces in hot oil about 15 minutes. Reduce heat; cover tightly. Cook 35 to 40 minutes more or till chicken is tender, uncovering skillet during the last 10 minutes.

For *mole verde,* in blender container combine tomatillos, green chili peppers, chicken broth, onion, walnuts, almonds, cilantro, the ¹/₄ teaspoon salt, and the dash pepper. Cover and blend till smooth. Heat sauce in saucepan; serve over chicken. Makes 3 or 4 servings.

Mole Poblano de Guajolote *Turkey Mole Puebla-Style*

1	4- to 5-pound turkey breast
1	teaspoon salt
	Water
2	tablespoons cooking oil
2	medium tomatoes, peeled, seeded, and chopped
1/2	cup chopped onion
2	canned green chili peppers, rinsed, seeded, and cut up
1/2	cup blanched almonds
1/3	cup raisins
1	6-inch tortilla, cut up
2	tablespoons sesame seed
1	clove garlic, minced
1/2	teaspoon crushed red pepper
1/4	teaspoon salt
1/4	teaspoon crushed *or* ground aniseed
1/4	teaspoon ground cloves
1/4	teaspoon ground cinnamon
1/4	teaspoon ground coriander seed
	Dash pepper
1/2	of a square (1/2 ounce) unsweetened chocolate, melted
	Toasted sesame seed

In large Dutch oven combine turkey breast, the 1 teaspoon salt, and enough water (about 10 cups) to cover. Bring to boiling; simmer 1 1/4 to 1 1/2 hours or till meat is tender. Drain, reserving 1 1/2 cups broth. Cool turkey slightly. Pat dry with paper toweling. In Dutch oven brown turkey breast in hot oil. Drain off fat.

To prepare *mole poblano,* in blender container combine reserved broth, tomatoes, onion, chili peppers, almonds, raisins, tortilla, sesame seed, garlic, red pepper, the 1/4 teaspoon salt, aniseed, cloves, cinnamon, coriander seed, and pepper. Cover and blend till nearly smooth. Stir in melted chocolate. Pour sauce over turkey breast in Dutch oven. Cover; simmer for 20 minutes or till heated through. To serve, slice turkey breast; arrange on platter, spooning sauce atop. Sprinkle with toasted sesame seed. Makes 8 to 10 servings.

About this recipe: Most famous of the *moles* is this one from Puebla. It intrigues the uninitiated with its imaginative sauce of chocolate and spices for turkey. Actually the word *mole* refers to a sauce cooked with chili peppers; the *mole* made with peanut butter is another popular version.

Pollo en Mole de Cacahuate *Chicken with Peanut Mole Sauce*

1	4-pound stewing chicken, cut up
8	cups water
4	stalks celery with leaves
1	medium carrot, sliced
1	small onion, cut up
2	sprigs parsley
2	teaspoons instant chicken bouillon granules
1/4	teaspoon pepper
1/2	of a 10-ounce can (2/3 cup) tomatoes with green chilies
2	slices white bread, torn
2	tablespoons creamy peanut butter
4	whole cloves
3	whole black peppercorns
1/2	inch stick cinnamon
3/4	teaspoon chili powder
1	small clove garlic, minced

Place chicken pieces in Dutch oven with water. Add celery, carrot, onion, parsley, bouillon granules, and pepper. Bring to boiling. Cover and cook over low heat 2 to 2 1/2 hours or till chicken is tender. Remove chicken pieces. Place in a 2-quart casserole. Strain broth; skim off fat. Reserve 1 1/2 cups of the broth for sauce (cover and refrigerate remaining broth for another use).

To prepare *mole de cacahuate,* in blender container place the reserved chicken broth, tomatoes with green chilies, bread, and peanut butter. Cover and blend till smooth. Turn into 2-quart saucepan. With mortar and pestle crush cloves, peppercorns, and cinnamon well; add to saucepan along with chili powder and garlic. Bring to boiling. Reduce heat and simmer, uncovered, 15 to 20 minutes or till thickened, stirring often.

Spoon *mole de cacahuate* over chicken in casserole. Bake, covered, in 350° oven 30 to 40 minutes or till heated through. Makes 6 to 8 servings.

Pescados *Fish and Seafood*

Pescado a la Naranja *Fish in Orange Juice*

2 pounds fresh *or* frozen halibut
    steaks *or* other fish steaks
1/2 cup finely chopped onion
2 cloves garlic, minced
2 tablespoons cooking oil
2 tablespoons snipped cilantro *or*
    parsley
1 teaspoon salt
1/8 teaspoon pepper
1/2 cup orange juice
1 tablespoon lemon juice
1 hard-cooked egg, cut in wedges

Thaw frozen fish. Arrange fish in a 12x7 1/2x2-inch baking dish. In small skillet cook onion and garlic in oil till onion is tender but not brown. Stir in cilantro or parsley, salt, and pepper. Spread mixture over fish. Combine orange juice and lemon juice; pour evenly over all. Bake, covered, in 400° oven for 20 to 25 minutes or till fish flakes easily when tested with a fork. Arrange egg wedges atop fish. Sprinkle with paprika and garnish with orange slices, if desired. Makes 6 servings.

Camarones en Escabeche *Marinated Shrimp in Avocado Halves*

12 ounces fresh *or* frozen shelled
    medium shrimp
2 tablespoons vinegar
1 1/2 teaspoons lemon juice
1/4 teaspoon salt
1/8 teaspoon dry mustard
    Dash pepper
1 small onion, thinly sliced
1 clove garlic, halved
3 tablespoons cooking oil
1 small pickled jalapeño pepper,
    rinsed, seeded, and cut in
    strips
2 avocados, halved and seeded
1 medium tomato, chopped

Thaw frozen shrimp. In bowl combine vinegar, lemon juice, salt, mustard, and pepper; set aside. In medium skillet cook shrimp, *half* of the onion slices, and the garlic in hot oil over medium-high heat 4 to 5 minutes or just till shrimp are done, stirring occasionally. Remove onion and garlic with slotted spoon; discard. Add shrimp and remaining oil to vinegar mixture in bowl along with remaining sliced onion and the jalapeño pepper. Cover and chill several hours or overnight, stirring occasionally.

    To serve, lift shrimp, onion slices, and jalapeño peppers from marinade; spoon into avocado halves. Sprinkle with chopped tomato; drizzle some of the marinade over all. Makes 4 servings.

Arroz con Jaibas *Rice with Crab*

3/4 cup long grain rice
1 small onion, finely chopped
1 small clove garlic, minced
2 tablespoons cooking oil
1 1/4 cups water
1 8-ounce can tomatoes, cut up
1 1/2 teaspoons instant chicken
    bouillon granules
1/4 teaspoon salt
    Bottled hot pepper sauce
1/2 cup frozen peas
1 7 1/2-ounce can crab meat,
    drained, broken in chunks,
    and cartilage removed *or* 1
    7-ounce package frozen
    shelled shrimp, cooked
2 tablespoons dry sherry

In skillet cook rice, onion, and garlic in oil over medium-low heat, stirring occasionally, till rice is golden brown. Remove from heat. Add water, *undrained* tomatoes, bouillon granules, salt, and a few dashes hot pepper sauce. Cover and simmer about 15 minutes or till most of liquid is absorbed. Stir in peas; cook 5 minutes more. Stir in crab or shrimp and sherry; heat through. Makes 4 servings.

Mexican waters yield abundant seafood for *Pescado a la Naranja*, *Arroz con Jaibas*, and *Camarones en Escabeche*.

Guisado de Ostiones *Oyster Stew with Vegetables*

1 pint shucked oysters
1 large onion, chopped
1 medium green bell pepper, chopped
1 clove garlic, minced
2 tablespoons butter *or* margarine
1 8-ounce can tomatoes, cut up
2 potatoes, peeled and chopped
1/2 cup sliced pimiento-stuffed olives
2 tablespoons capers
1 teaspoon salt
1/4 teaspoon dried marjoram, crushed
1/8 teaspoon ground cinnamon
Dash cayenne
2 teaspoons vinegar

Drain oysters, reserving liquid. Cut up any large oysters, if desired; set aside. In saucepan cook chopped onion, green pepper, and garlic in butter or margarine till tender. Stir in oyster liquid and *undrained* tomatoes; add potatoes, olives, capers, salt, marjoram, cinnamon, and cayenne. Bring to boiling. Reduce heat and simmer, covered, 10 to 15 minutes or till potatoes are nearly tender, stirring occasionally. Stir in oysters and vinegar. Simmer about 5 minutes longer or till oysters are done. Season to taste with additional salt and cayenne. Makes 4 servings.

Tortas de Camarón *Shrimp Fritters*

1 medium onion, finely chopped
1 clove garlic, minced
2 tablespoons cooking oil
1 8-ounce can tomatoes, cut up
1 4-ounce can green chili peppers, rinsed, seeded, and chopped
3/4 teaspoon salt
Dash pepper
3 egg whites
3 egg yolks
2 tablespoons all-purpose flour
1 4 1/2-ounce can shrimp, drained and chopped
Fat for frying

In saucepan cook onion and garlic in the 2 tablespoons oil till onion is tender. Stir in *undrained* tomatoes, chili peppers, 1/2 *teaspoon* of the salt, and pepper. Bring to boiling; reduce heat. Cover and simmer 20 minutes. Keep warm.

Meanwhile, beat egg whites till stiff peaks form. Beat yolks and remaining 1/4 teaspoon salt about 5 minutes or till thick and lemon-colored. Fold whites into yolks. Sprinkle flour atop; fold in. Fold in shrimp.

In deep skillet or saucepan heat 1 inch fat to 365°. Spoon shrimp mixture into the hot fat (use 2 tablespoons shrimp mixture for small fritters or 1/4 cup for larger ones). Fry about 2 minutes on each side or till golden brown. Drain on paper toweling. Serve hot with the tomato sauce. Makes twenty small or ten large fritters.

Escabeche de Pescado *Pickled Fish*

2 pounds fresh *or* frozen fish fillets
1/2 cup vinegar
1/4 cup cooking oil
1 4-ounce can green chili peppers, rinsed, seeded, and chopped
1 tablespoon finely shredded orange peel
1/4 cup orange juice
1/4 cup chopped onion
2 bay leaves
2 cloves garlic, minced
1 orange, thinly sliced

Thaw frozen fish. Place fish fillets in 10-inch skillet. Add boiling *water* to cover. Simmer, covered, 5 to 8 minutes or till fish flakes easily. Drain fish; arrange in a shallow baking dish. Combine vinegar, oil, chili peppers, orange peel, orange juice, onion, bay leaves, garlic, 1 teaspoon *salt,* and 1/8 teaspoon *pepper.* Pour over fish. Cover and refrigerate several hours or overnight. Drain off marinade; transfer fish to serving dish. Serve cold, garnished with orange slices. Makes 8 to 10 servings.

Pescado en Adobo Fish in Adobo Sauce

2 dried ancho chilies *or* ¹/₂
   teaspoon crushed red pepper
2 pounds fresh *or* frozen haddock
   fillets *or* other fish fillets
¹/₄ cup cooking oil
1 8-ounce can tomatoes
1 cup orange juice
2 medium onions, cut up
1 clove garlic, minced
1 teaspoon salt
¹/₂ teaspoon dried oregano,
   crushed
¹/₄ teaspoon ground cumin
¹/₄ teaspoon ground cinnamon
   Dash ground cloves
¹/₂ head lettuce, shredded
1 orange, thinly sliced
   Radish roses

Cut ancho chilies open; discard stems and seeds. Cut chilies into small pieces with scissors or a knife. Place in bowl; cover with boiling water. Let stand 45 to 60 minutes; drain. Meanwhile, thaw frozen fish. Lightly brown fish fillets on both sides in hot oil. Arrange fish in a 13x9x2-inch baking dish. Season with a little salt.

In blender container combine drained ancho chilies or red pepper with *undrained* tomatoes, orange juice, onions, garlic, salt, oregano, cumin, cinnamon, and cloves. Cover and blend till smooth. In the skillet used for cooking fish, simmer tomato mixture about 20 minutes, or till thickened, stirring occasionally. Pour over fish.

Bake, uncovered, in 350° oven for 30 minutes. Transfer fish to serving platter. Top with lettuce; garnish with orange slices and radish roses. Makes 6 servings.

Pescado Relleno Stuffed Fish

1 4-pound fresh *or* frozen dressed
   striped bass *or* other fish
2 cloves garlic
3 tablespoons lime juice
¹/₄ teaspoon pepper
1 medium onion, chopped (¹/₂ cup)
1 medium green bell pepper,
   chopped
2 tablespoons butter *or* margarine
2 medium tomatoes, peeled,
   seeded, and chopped
1 7¹/₂-ounce can (1¹/₂ cups) crab
   meat, drained, flaked, and
   cartilage removed
¹/₄ cup dry white wine

Thaw frozen fish. Cut fish in half lengthwise; remove bones. Cut garlic cloves; rub cut edge of garlic over all surfaces of the fish. Sprinkle with lime juice, pepper, and 1 teaspoon *salt*. Place *one half* of the fish in a well-greased 15x10x1-inch baking pan, skin side down.

In saucepan cook onion and green pepper in butter till onion is tender. Add tomatoes and ¹/₂ teaspoon *salt;* simmer, uncovered, 5 to 8 minutes or till very thick. Stir in crab and wine; heat through. Spoon crab mixture evenly over the halved fish in pan. Top with second half, skin side up.

Bake, covered, in 350° oven 45 to 50 minutes or till fish flakes easily with a fork. Makes 8 servings.

Pámpano Empapelado Pompano in Paper

6 fresh *or* frozen pompano fillets
   or other fish fillets
   Parchment *or* brown paper
¹/₂ cup chopped onion
¹/₂ teaspoon annatto seed, crushed
1 tablespoon cooking oil
¹/₄ cup orange juice
3 tablespoons lemon juice
1 2-ounce jar (¹/₄ cup) diced
   pimiento, drained
¹/₄ cup chopped pitted ripe olives
2 tablespoons snipped parsley
2 hard-cooked eggs, chopped

Thaw frozen fish. Cut parchment paper or brown paper into six 12-inch square pieces. Place 1 fillet on half of each piece of parchment. Sprinkle fish with salt.

In saucepan cook onion and annatto seed in oil till onion is tender. Stir in orange juice, lemon juice, pimiento, olives, and parsley. Simmer, covered, 5 minutes. Add hard-cooked eggs. Spoon 3 tablespoons sauce over each fillet. Fold parchment over fillet. Seal by turning edges up and folding. Place packets in 15x10x1-inch baking pan. Bake in 350° oven for 20 to 25 minutes or till fish is done. Cut packets open with large X on top; fold back each segment. Transfer paper packets to dinner plates. Garnish with shredded lettuce and sliced radishes, if desired. Makes 6 servings.

Huachinango a la Veracruzana *Red Snapper Veracruz-Style*

6 fresh *or* frozen red snapper
    fillets or other fish fillets
    (2 pounds)
12 small new potatoes (1 pound)
1/3 cup all-purpose flour
1 teaspoon salt
1/8 teaspoon pepper
1/4 cup olive oil *or* cooking oil
1 large onion, sliced
1 clove garlic, minced
1 15-ounce can tomato puree
1/2 cup sliced pimiento-stuffed
    olives
1/4 cup water
1 tablespoon lime juice
1 small pickled jalapeño pepper,
    rinsed, seeded, and cut in
    strips (optional)
1/2 teaspoon sugar
1/8 teaspoon ground cinnamon
1/8 teaspoon ground cloves
1 bay leaf
    Buttered toast (optional)

Thaw frozen fish. In covered pan cook potatoes in enough boiling salted water to cover for about 15 minutes or till nearly tender; drain. When cool enough to handle, peel and set aside.

Combine flour, salt, and pepper. Coat fish fillets on both sides with flour mixture. In a large skillet cook fish fillets in hot oil about 5 minutes per side or till done. Remove from skillet; set aside. Drain off oil, reserving 1 tablespoon.

In same skillet cook onion and garlic in reserved oil till tender but not brown. Add tomato puree, olives, water, lime juice, jalapeño pepper, sugar, cinnamon, cloves, and bay leaf; mix well. Add potatoes; bring to boiling. Reduce heat and simmer, uncovered, for 5 minutes. Add fish fillets; cook about 5 minutes or till heated through. Remove bay leaf. Arrange fish and potatoes on serving platter; spoon sauce atop. Garnish platter with triangles of buttered toast, if desired. Makes 6 servings.

Pescado Borracho *Drunken Fish*

1 3-pound dressed fresh *or* frozen
    red snapper *or* other fish
2 dried ancho chilies *or*
    1/2 teaspoon crushed
    red pepper
1/3 cup dry red wine
1/2 cup chopped onion
1 clove garlic, minced
2 tablespoons olive oil *or* cooking
    oil
3 medium tomatoes, peeled,
    seeded, and chopped
1/3 cup water
1/4 cup snipped parsley
1 teaspoon sugar
1/2 teaspoon salt
1/2 teaspoon dried oregano,
    crushed
1/4 teaspoon ground cumin
    Salt and pepper
1/2 cup sliced pimiento-stuffed
    olives
1 tablespoon capers (optional)

Thaw frozen fish. Cut chilies open. Discard stems and seeds. Cut chilies into small pieces with scissors or a knife. Place snipped chilies in small bowl; add boiling water to cover. Let stand 45 to 60 minutes; drain. Place chilies in blender container; add wine. Blend till nearly smooth.

In medium saucepan cook onion and garlic in hot oil till tender but not brown. Add chili-wine mixture (*or* add crushed red pepper to saucepan along with wine), to-matoes, 1/3 cup water, parsley, sugar, salt, oregano, and cumin. Bring to boiling; reduce heat. Cover and simmer 5 minutes.

Meanwhile, place fish in greased 13x9x2-inch baking dish. Season cavity of fish with salt and pepper. Stir olives and capers into tomato sauce; pour over fish. Cover; bake in 350° oven for 45 to 60 minutes or till fish flakes easily when tested with fork. Carefully remove fish to serving plat-ter. Pass sauce. Makes 6 to 8 servings.

Pescado en Cilantro Fish in Cilantro Sauce

6 fresh *or* frozen red snapper
  fillets or other fish fillets
  (2 pounds)
1 small onion, sliced
1 small clove garlic, minced
1 tablespoon cooking oil
1/4 cup toasted almonds, ground
2 tablespoons lime juice
1/2 of a pickled jalapeño pepper,
  rinsed, seeded, and chopped
  (1 1/2 teaspoons)
1/2 teaspoon salt
  Dash pepper
  Salt
1/2 cup snipped cilantro *or* parsley

Thaw frozen fish. Cook onion and garlic in oil till tender but not brown. Add the almonds, lime juice, jalapeño pepper, the 1/2 teaspoon salt, and pepper. Heat through.

In a well-greased 13x9x2-inch baking dish arrange fish fillets; sprinkle lightly with salt. Top with onion mixture. Sprinkle evenly with cilantro or parsley.

Bake, covered, in 350° oven for 40 minutes or till fish flakes easily with a fork. Makes 6 servings.

Pipián de Camarones Shrimp with Pumpkin-Seed Sauce

1 pound fresh *or* frozen shelled
  shrimp
1/2 cup finely chopped onion
1 clove garlic, minced
2 tablespoons cooking oil
2 tablespoons all-purpose flour
1 8-ounce can tomatoes, cut up
1 pickled jalapeño pepper, rinsed,
  seeded, and finely chopped
1 1/2 teaspoons ground coriander
  seed
1 teaspoon salt
1/2 teaspoon instant chicken
  bouillon granules
1/2 teaspoon sugar
1/2 cup toasted, salted pumpkin
  seeds, coarsely chopped
2 tablespoons lime juice
  Hot cooked rice

Thaw frozen shrimp. In large skillet cook onion and garlic in oil till tender but not brown; stir in flour. Add *undrained* tomatoes, chopped jalapeño pepper, coriander, salt, bouillon granules, and sugar. Cook and stir till thickened and bubbly. Stir in shrimp. Cover and simmer 10 minutes or till shrimp is done, stirring frequently. Stir in pumpkin seeds and lime juice; heat through. Serve over hot cooked rice. Makes 4 servings.

Bacalao a la Vizcaina Spanish-Style Codfish

1 pound salt cod
1 small onion, chopped
1 clove garlic, minced
1/4 cup cooking oil
1 8-ounce can tomatoes, cut up
2 tablespoons chopped pimiento
  Dash pepper
2 tablespoons dry sherry
1/4 cup sliced pimiento-stuffed
  olives

Rinse excess salt from cod; then soak cod overnight in cold water, changing water several times. Drain and cut into serving-size pieces.

Cook onion and garlic in oil till onion is tender but not brown. Add fish pieces and cook till lightly browned. Add *undrained* tomatoes, pimiento, and pepper. Simmer, covered, about 20 minutes or till fish is tender. Add sherry; heat through. Garnish with olives. Makes 4 or 5 servings.

Huevos Eggs

Tortilla a la Mexicana Mexican Omelet with Chicken

¹/₂ cup water
1 medium tomato, peeled and
    seeded
1 tablespoon cooking oil
2 teaspoons chili powder
1 teaspoon instant chicken
    bouillon granules
1 cup chopped cooked chicken *or*
    turkey
8 eggs
¹/₄ cup water
¹/₂ teaspoon salt
¹/₈ teaspoon pepper
4 tablespoons butter *or* margarine

In blender container combine the ¹/₂ cup water, tomato, oil, chili powder, and chicken bouillon granules; blend till smooth. Transfer to a small saucepan. Cook, stirring constantly, about 7 minutes or till mixture thickens. Stir in chicken. Season with a little salt and pepper. Keep warm.

With a fork beat eggs with the ¹/₄ cup water, salt, and pepper till blended but not frothy. In an 8-inch skillet or omelet pan heat *1 tablespoon* of the butter until it sizzles and browns lightly. Tilt pan to coat sides. Pour in about ¹/₂ *cup* of egg mixture, leaving heat moderately high. As egg begins to set on bottom, lift edges allowing uncooked portion to flow under. Continue until all egg is cooked. Spoon about ¹/₄ *cup* of chicken filling down center of omelet. Fold sides over filling. Tilt pan and roll omelet onto a hot plate. Repeat with remaining butter, egg mixture, and chicken filling three more times. Makes 4 servings.

Tortilla Española Spanish Omelet

2 large potatoes, peeled and
    finely chopped (3 cups)
1 medium onion, finely chopped
³/₄ teaspoon salt
¹/₄ teaspoon pequin chilies,
    crushed *or* ¹/₄ teaspoon
    crushed red pepper
2 tablespoons cooking oil
6 beaten eggs
¹/₃ cup milk
¹/₂ teaspoon salt
¹/₈ teaspoon pepper

Combine potatoes, onion, the ³/₄ teaspoon salt, and crushed chilies. Heat oil in 10-inch ovenware skillet. Add potato mixture to skillet; cover and cook over medium heat 12 to 15 minutes or till tender, stirring occasionally.

Combine eggs, milk, the ¹/₂ teaspoon salt, and pepper; pour over potatoes in skillet. Reduce heat; cover and cook over low heat 8 to 10 minutes or till eggs are nearly set. Uncover skillet and place under broiler 3 to 4 inches from heat 2 to 3 minutes or just till top is set. Serves 4 to 6.

About these two recipes: In Mexico, the word *tortilla* has two food meanings. Although the versatile corn or flour pancake is more familiar, omelets are also called *tortillas*.

Huevos Girasol Sunflower Eggs

1¹/₂ cups fine noodles (3 ounces)
2 tablespoons cooking oil
³/₄ cup chopped onion
1 clove garlic, minced
4 large tomatoes, peeled, cored,
    and chopped (3 cups)
1 4-ounce can green chili
    peppers, rinsed, seeded, and
    chopped
4 teaspoons sugar
4 teaspoons vinegar
1 teaspoon salt
¹/₄ teaspoon ground cinnamon
¹/₈ teaspoon ground cloves
1 tablespoon cooking oil
6 eggs
1 tablespoon water
1 avocado

In medium skillet cook noodles in the 2 tablespoons hot oil 3 to 4 minutes or till lightly browned, stirring constantly. Remove noodles from skillet, reserving oil; set noodles aside. Cook onion and garlic in reserved oil till tender. Stir in tomatoes, chili peppers, sugar, vinegar, salt, cinnamon, and cloves. Bring to boiling; reduce heat. Boil gently, uncovered, about 15 minutes or till slightly thickened, stirring occasionally.

Meanwhile, cook the browned noodles in large amount of boiling salted water till tender, 7 to 8 minutes; drain.

In skillet heat the 1 tablespoon oil. Carefully break eggs into skillet; sprinkle with a little salt and pepper. When whites are set and edges cooked, add the 1 tablespoon water. Cover skillet and cook eggs to desired doneness.

Combine noodles and *half* of the tomato sauce; transfer to platter. Arrange eggs atop noodles. Spoon remaining tomato mixture over. Seed, peel, and slice avocado. Arrange slices sunburst-fashion over eggs. Serves 6.

Saying *buenas dias* with *Huevos Rancheros* makes it a very good morning indeed. These Ranch-Style Eggs use tortillas and a not-too-spicy sauce as the base for cheese-topped eggs.

Huevos Rancheros *Ranch-Style Eggs*

2 **tablespoons cooking oil**
6 **6-inch tortillas**
½ **cup chopped onion**
1 **clove garlic, minced**
3 **large tomatoes, peeled, cored and chopped**
1 **4-ounce can green chili peppers, rinsed, seeded, and chopped**
¼ **teaspoon salt**
1 **tablespoon cooking oil**
6 **eggs**
1 **cup shredded monterey jack cheese (4 ounces)**

In small skillet heat 2 tablespoons oil. Holding tortillas with tongs, dip one at a time in hot oil for 10 seconds or till limp. Line a 10x6x2-inch baking dish with tortillas. Keep warm. In same skillet cook the onion and garlic till tender but not brown (add more oil if necessary). Stir in tomatoes, green chili peppers, and salt. Simmer, uncovered, for 10 minutes. Spoon over tortillas.

In large skillet heat 1 tablespoon oil. Carefully break eggs into skillet; sprinkle with salt and pepper. When whites are set and edges cooked, add 1 tablespoon *water*. Cover skillet and cook eggs to desired doneness.

Carefully arrange cooked eggs over sauce in baking dish. Sprinkle with cheese. Place under broiler for 1 to 2 minutes or till cheese melts. Serve at once. Serves 6.

Huevos Revueltos   *Scrambled Eggs*

1 cup Salsa de Chile Verde (see page 16)
6 slightly beaten eggs
Dairy sour cream

In 10-inch skillet heat Salsa de Chile Verde over medium heat till bubbly. Pour beaten eggs over sauce in skillet. Cook without stirring over low heat for 1 to 1½ minutes or till mixture begins to set on bottom. Lift and fold eggs with spatula so uncooked part runs to bottom. Continue lifting and folding about 5 minutes more till eggs are cooked through, but still glossy and moist. Pass sour cream to spoon on top. Makes 3 or 4 servings.

Huevos Revueltos con Chorizo   *Scrambled Eggs with Sausage*

4 ounces chorizo *or* Italian sausage
6 eggs
¼ cup milk
¼ teaspoon salt
Dash pepper
1 medium tomato, peeled, seeded, and chopped

Remove casing from sausage and crumble into an unheated 10-inch skillet. Slowly cook sausage for 15 to 20 minutes, stirring occasionally. Drain off excess fat. In a bowl beat eggs, milk, salt, and pepper with a fork.

Pour egg mixture over sausage in skillet. Cook without stirring over low heat till eggs start to set on bottom and sides of pan. Lift and fold eggs with spatula so uncooked part runs to bottom. Continue lifting and folding for 2 to 3 minutes or till eggs start to set. Fold in the chopped tomato. Continue lifting and folding 2 to 3 minutes more or till eggs are cooked through but still glossy and moist. Makes 4 servings.

Huevos Revueltos con Calabacitas   *Scrambled Eggs with Zucchini*

1 cup coarsely chopped zucchini
2 tablespoons butter *or* margarine
6 eggs
¼ cup milk
½ teaspoon chili powder
¼ teaspoon salt
Dash pepper
½ cup shredded monterey jack cheese (2 ounces)

In medium skillet cook zucchini in butter or margarine for 4 to 5 minutes or till almost tender. In bowl beat eggs, milk, chili powder, salt, and pepper with a fork. Stir in *half* of the cheese.

Pour egg mixture over zucchini in skillet. Cook without stirring over low heat till eggs start to set on bottom and sides of pan. Lift and fold eggs with spatula so uncooked part runs to bottom. Continue lifting and folding about 5 minutes more or till eggs are cooked through but still glossy and moist. Sprinkle with remaining cheese. Serves 4.

Huevos Revueltos con Nopalitos   *Scrambled Eggs with Cactus*

1 8-ounce can nopalitos (cactus pieces), drained and rinsed
1 tablespoon chopped onion
2 tablespoons butter *or* margarine
8 eggs
⅓ cup milk
¼ teaspoon salt
Dash pepper

In 10-inch skillet cook cactus pieces and onion in butter or margarine till onion is tender but not brown. In bowl beat eggs, milk, salt, and pepper with a fork.

Pour egg mixture over cactus pieces and onion in skillet. Cook without stirring over low heat till eggs start to set on bottom and sides of pan. Lift and fold eggs with spatula so uncooked part runs to bottom. Continue lifting and folding about 5 minutes more or till eggs are cooked through but still glossy and moist. Makes 6 servings.

Chiles Rellenos *Stuffed Chilies*

8 green bell peppers *or* large
    poblano chilies
1 16-ounce can tomatoes
1 small onion, cut up
1 teaspoon instant beef bouillon
    granules
    Dash pepper
    Dash ground cinnamon
4 cups shredded monterey jack *or*
    cheddar cheese (1 pound) *or* 4
    cups Picadillo, heated (see
    page 18)
8 egg yolks
2 tablespoons water
1/4 cup all-purpose flour
1/2 teaspoon salt
8 egg whites
    Fat for frying
    Cilantro *or* parsley

Broil peppers 2 inches from heat for about 15 minutes, turning often, till all sides are blistered. Place peppers in a paper or plastic bag. Close bag and let stand about 10 minutes or till cool enough to handle.

Meanwhile, make tomato sauce. In blender container combine *undrained* tomatoes, onion, bouillon granules, pepper, and cinnamon. Cover; blend till smooth. Transfer to a saucepan. Heat to boiling; simmer, uncovered, for 5 minutes. Cover and keep warm over low heat while preparing peppers.

Peel peppers; remove stems and seeds. Stuff each pepper with 1/2 *cup* of the cheese or 1/2 *cup* hot Picadillo. Set aside. Slightly beat egg yolks and water. Add flour and salt; beat 6 minutes or till thick and lemon-colored. Beat egg whites till stiff peaks form. Fold yolks into whites.

In a large heavy skillet heat 1/2 inch fat to 375°. For each serving spoon about 1/3 cup egg batter into hot fat, spreading batter in a circle. Fry 3 or 4 at a time. As batter begins to set, gently top each mound with a stuffed chili. Cover with another 1/3 cup batter. Continue cooking 2 to 3 minutes more, till underside is brown. Turn carefully; brown second side. Drain on paper toweling; keep warm in 300° oven while preparing remainder. Serve with tomato sauce; garnish with snipped cilantro or parsley. Makes 8 servings.

About this recipe: The chilies in the recipe title are poblano chilies, large, mild-flavored green peppers available in Mexican markets (see page 10 for more information). Green bell peppers can be easily substituted.

Huevos Motuleños *Eggs Motul-Style*

1 1/4 cups dry black beans (8 ounces)
3 cups water
1/4 cup chopped onion
1 clove garlic, minced
1 teaspoon salt
1/4 teaspoon dried epazote,
    crushed (optional)
1 8-ounce can tomatoes, finely
    chopped
2 tablespoons finely chopped
    onion
1/2 teaspoon salt
1/8 teaspoon cayenne
    Cooking oil
1 10-ounce package frozen peas
1 1/2 cups chopped ham
8 6-inch tortillas
8 eggs
1/2 cup shredded monterey jack
    cheese (2 ounces)

In large saucepan soak beans overnight in 3 cups water. (Or, bring to boiling; simmer 2 minutes. Cover and let stand 1 hour.) Do not drain. Add the 1/4 cup onion, garlic, the 1 teaspoon salt, and epazote; cook for 2 hours or till very tender.

Combine *undrained* tomatoes, the 2 tablespoons chopped onion, 1/2 teaspoon salt, and cayenne. Set aside.

Heat *2 tablespoons* cooking oil in large heavy skillet. Add beans with liquid. Mash beans in skillet. Cook, uncovered, over medium heat 3 to 5 minutes or till very thick.

Cook peas according to package directions; drain. Toss with ham; cover and keep warm. Heat 1/4 inch cooking oil in another heavy skillet. Fry tortillas 20 to 40 seconds per side or till crisp and golden. Drain on paper toweling. Spread about 1/3 cup bean mixture on each tortilla; keep warm in 300° oven.

In same oil fry eggs till set. Season with salt and pepper. Place one atop each bean-covered tortilla. Sprinkle each with about 1/2 cup of the ham mixture. Spoon some tomato sauce on top. Sprinkle with cheese. Makes 8 servings.

Otras Cosas

Broaden your cooking ventures by sampling these enticing "other things"— the breads, desserts, vegetables, salads, and beverages that complete a Mexican menu.

The favorable climate that grows corn for cornmeal also produces wheat for outstanding breads plus a bountiful harvest of vegetables and fruits to enjoy fresh or in cooked dishes.

Start out with big, sweet buns to enjoy with your breakfast coffee, or try your hand at the spindle-shaped hard rolls. Well-seasoned "beans in a pot" and vegetable fritters await your discovery, too. On the sweet side are fruit puddings, delicate custard concoctions, and fluffy meringue desserts, along with some traditional candies. Recipes for hot chocolate drinks and fruit-studded punches are delicious thirst-quenchers to round out the chapter.

Pictured clockwise are *Bizcochos, Chocolate Mexicano, Bolillos,* and long, crisp *Churros* (see index for page numbers).

Legumbres y Ensaladas
Vegetables and Salads

Frijoles Blancos *White Beans*

1¼ cups dry white *or* navy beans (8 ounces)
4 slices bacon, cut up
½ teaspoon salt
1 16-ounce can tomatoes
1 small onion, quartered
¾ teaspoon salt
½ teaspoon sugar
⅛ teaspoon pepper
2 cups coarsely chopped cabbage
1 cup finely chopped cooked pork (optional)
1 link chorizo *or* Italian sausage, cooked and chopped
1 whole clove
⅛ teaspoon saffron, crushed

In large bowl soak beans overnight in 4 cups *water*. (Or, in saucepan bring beans and water to boiling; simmer 2 minutes. Cover and let stand 1 hour.) Do not drain. In large saucepan cook beans with bacon and the ½ teaspoon salt for 1½ hours or till beans are tender.

In blender container place *undrained* tomatoes, onion, the ¾ teaspoon salt, sugar, and pepper. Cover; blend till smooth. Stir into beans along with cabbage, pork, sausage, clove, and saffron. Bring to boiling. Simmer 12 to 15 minutes or just till cabbage is tender. Do not overcook cabbage. Season to taste. Serve at once. Makes 4 to 6 servings.

Sopa Seca de Tortilla *Tortilla Casserole*

10 6-inch tortillas
Cooking oil
2 green bell peppers, cut in strips
1 medium onion, chopped (½ cup)
1 clove garlic, minced
1 teaspoon salt
1 cup whipping cream
1 cup shredded monterey jack cheese (4 ounces)

Cut tortillas in strips about 3 inches long and ½ inch wide. In medium skillet heat ¼ inch of oil. Fry tortilla strips, a few at a time, about 10 seconds or just till limp. Remove with slotted spoon. Drain on paper toweling.

Pour off all but about 2 tablespoons oil from skillet. Add green pepper strips, onion, and garlic; cook till onion is tender. Sprinkle vegetables with salt. In 1½-quart casserole stir together tortilla strips, vegetables, whipping cream, and *half* of the cheese. Cover and bake in 350° oven for 20 minutes. Uncover. Stir gently; sprinkle with remaining cheese. Bake, uncovered, about 10 minutes more or till heated through. Makes 6 servings.

About this recipe: Soups in name only, the *sopa secas* or dry soups of Mexico are mainly rice, noodles, bread, or tortillas. Some contain meat while others include vegetables, serving as both pasta and vegetable at mealtime.

Arroz con Tomate *Spanish Rice (photo on page 19)*

½ cup chopped green bell pepper
¼ cup chopped onion
1 clove garlic, minced
½ teaspoon dried basil, crushed
½ teaspoon dried rosemary, crushed
2 tablespoons olive oil *or* cooking oil
1 cup long grain rice
1 cup chopped, peeled tomato
1 teaspoon salt
⅛ teaspoon pepper

In skillet cook green pepper, onion, garlic, basil, and rosemary in hot oil till vegetables are tender. Stir in rice, chopped tomato, salt, pepper, and 2 cups *water*. Cook, covered, over low heat for about 20 minutes or till rice is done. Makes 6 servings.

Shown are *Ensalada de Jícama, Ensalada de Ejotes* (see page 77), *Frijoles Blancos,* and *Sopa Seca de Tortilla.*

Zanahorias en Tortitas *Carrot Fritters*

¹/₂ **pound carrots, cut up (about 2 cups)**
2 **tablespoons chopped onion**
1 **cup water**
1 **tablespoon snipped parsley**
1 **cup all-purpose flour**
1 **tablespoon baking powder**
³/₄ **teaspoon salt**
1 **beaten egg**
 Fat for frying
 Mustard Sauce (optional)

In small covered saucepan cook carrots and onion in water about 25 minutes or till tender. Drain, reserving ¹/₂ cup cooking liquid. Finely chop carrots. Toss parsley with cooked vegetables and set aside. In mixing bowl stir together flour, baking powder, and salt; add egg and reserved liquid. Stir just till moistened; fold in vegetables. Carefully drop batter by rounded tablespoons into 2 to 3 tablespoons hot fat; cook about 2 minutes on each side or till golden. (*Or*, cook 3¹/₂ to 4 minutes in 1¹/₂ inches hot fat (365°), turning once.) Drain. Serve plain or with Mustard Sauce. Makes 24.

Mustard Sauce: In small mixing bowl combine ¹/₄ cup *prepared mustard*, 2 tablespoons *wine vinegar*, ¹/₄ teaspoon *salt,* and dash *pepper*. Using electric mixer or rotary beater, beat in 2 tablespoons cooking *oil*, a tablespoon at a time.

Frijoles Borraohitos *Beans with Beer*

1¹/₄ **cups dry red, pink,** *or* **pinto beans (8 ounces)**
4 **cups water**
1 **12-ounce can beer**
¹/₂ **cup chopped onion**
6 **slices bacon**
1 **8-ounce can tomatoes, cut up**
1 **tablespoon snipped cilantro** *or* **parsley**
1 **teaspoon salt**
¹/₂ **teaspoon crushed red pepper**

In large saucepan soak beans overnight in 4 cups water. (Or bring beans and water to boiling; simmer 2 minutes. Cover and let stand 1 hour.) Do not drain. Add beer and onion. Bring to boiling; cover and simmer mixture for about 1¹/₂ hours or till beans are tender.

Cook bacon till crisp; drain and crumble. Add bacon to bean mixture along with *undrained* tomatoes, cilantro or parsley, salt, and crushed red pepper; cover and simmer 30 minutes more. Makes 4 servings.

Frijoles de Olla *Beans in a Pot*

1 **pound dry pinto, white,** *or* **pink beans (2¹/₂ cups)**
6 **cups water**
3 **cloves garlic, minced**
1 **large onion, chopped (1 cup)**
1 **pickled jalapeño pepper, rinsed, seeded, and finely chopped**
1¹/₂ **teaspoons salt**

In large kettle or Dutch oven soak beans overnight in 6 cups water. (Or bring to boiling; simmer 2 minutes. Cover and let stand 1 hour.) Do not drain. Add garlic, onion, chopped jalapeño pepper, and salt to the beans. Bring mixture to boiling; simmer for 1¹/₂ to 2 hours or until beans are tender. Makes 8 to 10 servings.

Budín de Elote *Corn Pudding*

4 **or 5 ears fresh corn**
3 **egg yolks**
2 **tablespoons butter, melted**
2 **tablespoons sugar**
1 **teaspoon salt**
2 **cups milk**
3 **stiffly beaten egg whites**

With sharp knife make cuts down center of each row of corn kernels. Scrape cobs; measure 1³/₄ cups cut corn.

Beat egg yolks about 5 minutes or till thick and lemon-colored. Stir in corn, butter, sugar, and salt. Slowly blend in milk. Fold in the stiffly beaten egg whites. Turn into 8x8x2-inch baking dish. Bake in 350° oven for 45 to 50 minutes or till set. Makes 6 to 8 servings.

Legumbres a la Española *Spanish Vegetables*

2 large ears fresh corn
1/2 cup finely chopped onion
1 clove garlic, minced
1 tablespoon olive *or* cooking oil
1 pound zucchini, sliced
2 cups chopped, peeled tomatoes
1 teaspoon dried oregano, crushed
1 teaspoon salt
1/8 teaspoon pepper

With sharp knife cut kernels from ears of corn to measure 1 cup; *do not scrape cob.* In skillet cook onion and garlic in oil till onion is tender but not brown. Stir in corn, zucchini, tomatoes, oregano, salt, and pepper. Cover and cook over low heat for about 15 minutes or till tender. Serve in bowls. Makes 4 to 6 servings.

Elote en Tortitas *Corn Fritters*

3 or 4 ears fresh corn *or* 1
    8³/4-ounce can whole kernel
    corn
Milk
1¹/2 cups all-purpose flour
1 tablespoon baking powder
3/4 teaspoon salt
1 beaten egg
Fat for frying

With sharp knife make cuts down center of each row of corn kernels. Scrape cobs; measure 1 cup corn. Drain cut or canned corn, reserving liquid. Add enough milk to corn liquid to measure 1 cup. Stir together flour, baking powder, and salt. Combine egg, milk mixture, and corn; add to dry ingredients. Mix just till moistened. Carefully drop batter by tablespoons into 2 to 3 tablespoons hot fat; cook about 2 minutes on each side or till golden. (*Or*, cook 3¹/2 to 4 minutes in 1¹/2 inches hot fat (365°), turning once.) Drain on paper toweling. Makes 24.

Calabaza Enmielada *Squash in Syrup*

3 to 4 pounds pumpkin, banana
    squash, *or* other winter
    squash, cut in wedges
3/4 cup packed dark brown sugar
2 tablespoons water
2 tablespoons butter *or* margarine
Milk (optional)

Remove seeds from squash wedges. Pack sugar into the cavities of the squash. Place water in large, heavy skillet, arrange squash pieces, rind side down, in single layer in skillet. Dot with butter. Cover pan tightly; cook over low heat for 20 to 30 minutes or till squash is tender. Scoop squash from rinds into serving bowl; pour syrup from pan over. Pass milk to pour over each serving. Serves 6 to 8.

Eye-Catching Vegetables

Mexican cooks take full advantage of the beauty and appeal of cooked and raw vegetables. The secret—don't relegate vegetables to a separate bowl. Instead, put their bright colors to work right on the entrée platter to make even the humblest dish irresistible.
- Encircle sliced chicken or pork with cooked carrot rounds and radish roses.
- Stir a small amount of green peas into rice or soup combinations that might otherwise lack color.
- Add a handful of shredded cabbage or lettuce at the last minute to enhance hot or cold entrées.
- Decorate a full platter or a single serving with thin slices of avocado. Place slices in a row or arrange them sunburst-fashion.

Colorful *Ensalada de Noche Buena* gives a festive look to the Christmas Eve buffet table. A liberal sprinkling of peanuts and pomegranate seeds is the finishing touch.

Ensalada de Noche Buena   *Christmas Eve Salad*

1 **fresh pineapple** *or* **1 20-ounce can pineapple chunks**
2 **large oranges**
2 **medium bananas**
1 **large apple**
3 **medium beets, cooked, peeled, and sliced** *or* **1 16-ounce can sliced beets, drained**
1 **jicama, peeled and sliced (optional)**
1 **stick sugar cane, peeled and chopped (optional)**
  Lettuce
½ **cup peanuts**
  Pomegranate seeds
  Mayonnaise *or* **salad dressing**
  Milk

Remove crown of fresh pineapple. Peel pineapple and remove eyes; quarter and remove core. Cut pineapple into chunks. (Or, drain canned pineapple.)

Peel oranges; section over a bowl to catch juice. Peel and slice bananas. Core and slice apple. Toss apple and banana with orange sections and orange juice.

Drain fruits; arrange with pineapple chunks, sliced beets, jicama, and sugar cane on large lettuce-lined platter. Sprinkle with peanuts and pomegranate seeds. Thin mayonnaise or salad dressing with a little milk to make drizzling consistency. Pass with salad. Makes 6 to 8 servings.

Ensalada de Goliflor *Cauliflower Salad*

1 medium head cauliflower
2 cups Guacamole (see page 17)
   or 2 6-ounce cartons frozen
   avocado dip, thawed
¹/₂ cup shredded monterey jack *or*
   cheddar cheese (2 ounces)
   Radish roses

Remove leaves and core from cauliflower. In covered saucepan cook whole cauliflower in small amount of boiling salted water 20 to 25 minutes or till just tender when tested with a fork. Drain well and chill. Place chilled cauliflower on platter. Spread Guacamole over entire surface. Sprinkle with cheese. Garnish platter with radish roses. Makes 6 to 8 servings.

Ensalada de Ejotes *Green Bean Salad (photo on page 73)*

1 pound green beans, cut in
   1-inch pieces (3 cups) *or* 1
   16-ounce can cut green
   beans, drained
¹/₃ cup olive oil *or* cooking oil
1 2-ounce jar sliced pimiento,
   drained
2 tablespoons vinegar
2 tablespoons lemon juice
1 tablespoon minced onion
1 tablespoon snipped parsley
2 teaspoons sugar
¹/₂ teaspoon salt
¹/₈ teaspoon freshly ground black
   pepper

In covered saucepan cook fresh beans in a small amount of boiling salted water about 20 minutes or till tender; drain. In screw-top jar combine oil, pimiento, vinegar, lemon juice, onion, parsley, sugar, salt, and pepper. Cover and shake till well blended. Toss with cooked or canned green beans. Cover and chill. Drain beans. Serve on a bed of lettuce, if desired. Makes 4 or 5 servings.

Ensalada de Galabacita *Zucchini Salad*

4 cups sliced zucchini
1 cup white wine vinegar
³/₄ cup olive oil *or* cooking oil
2 tablespoons sugar
1 clove garlic, minced
1 teaspoon dried basil, crushed
1 teaspoon salt
   Few dashes pepper
   Lettuce
¹/₄ cup sliced green onion
2 medium tomatoes, cut in thin
   wedges

Cook zucchini in a small amount of boiling salted water for about 3 minutes or till crisp-tender; drain. Arrange *half* the zucchini in a single layer in 10x6x2-inch dish.

In screw-top jar combine vinegar, oil, sugar, garlic, basil, salt, and pepper. Cover and shake well. Pour *half* the dressing over zucchini in dish. Top with remaining zucchini and dressing. Cover and chill overnight.

To serve, drain zucchini; reserve ¹/₄ cup dressing. Arrange zucchini on lettuce-lined plate; top with sliced green onion. Arrange tomato wedges around zucchini; drizzle with the reserved dressing. Makes 8 servings.

Ensalada de Jícama *Jicama Salad (photo on page 73)*

8 ounces jicama, peeled and
   cubed (1¹/₂ cups)
1 large cucumber, sliced
1 orange, peeled and cubed
2 tablespoons lemon juice
³/₄ teaspoon chili powder
   Salt

In large bowl combine jicama, cucumber, and orange. Sprinkle with lemon juice and chili powder; toss to coat. Cover and chill at least 2 hours. Just before serving, sprinkle lightly with salt; toss. Sprinkle lightly with additional chili powder, if desired. Makes 6 servings.

Panes y Postres *Breads and Desserts*

Pan Dulce *Sweet Rolls*

3¹/₂ to 4 cups all-purpose flour
1 package active dry yeast
1 cup milk
¹/₄ cup sugar
¹/₄ cup shortening
1 teaspoon salt
2 eggs
²/₃ cup all-purpose flour
¹/₂ cup sugar
¹/₄ cup butter *or* margarine
2 beaten egg yolks
¹/₄ teaspoon vanilla

In large mixer bowl combine *2 cups* of the flour and the yeast. In saucepan heat milk, the ¹/₄ cup sugar, shortening, and salt till warm (115° to 120°), stirring constantly. Add to dry mixture in bowl; add whole eggs. Beat at low speed of electric mixer for ¹/₂ minute, scraping bowl. Beat 3 minutes at high speed. By hand stir in enough remaining flour (1¹/₂ to 2 cups) to make moderately stiff dough.

Knead dough on lightly floured surface 8 to 10 minutes or till smooth. Place in greased bowl; turn once to grease surface. Cover; let rise 1 to 1¹/₄ hours or till double. Punch down. Divide into 16 equal pieces; shape each into a smooth ball. Roll or pat each into 3-inch circle. Place 2 inches apart on greased baking sheet.

Combine the ²/₃ cup flour and the ¹/₂ cup sugar. Cut in butter with pastry blender to make fine, even crumbs. With a fork stir in egg yolks and vanilla. Mix with hands till well blended. Divide mixture into 16 portions. With rolling pin roll each to a 3-inch circle on a lightly floured surface. With spatula transfer each to a circle of dough on baking sheet. Slash top into squares, circles, or shell forms. Cover and let rise about 30 minutes or till double. Bake in 375° oven for 15 to 18 minutes. Makes 16.

Rosca de Reyes *Three Kings' Bread*

3 to 3¹/₂ cups all-purpose flour
1 package active dry yeast
²/₃ cup milk
6 tablespoons butter *or* margarine
¹/₃ cup granulated sugar
1 teaspoon salt
2 eggs
2 tablespoons butter *or* margarine, melted
2 tablespoons granulated sugar
¹/₂ teaspoon ground cinnamon
¹/₂ cup chopped blanched almonds
¹/₂ cup chopped mixed candied fruits and peels
¹/₂ cup sifted powdered sugar
¹/₄ teaspoon vanilla
Milk
2 tablespoons finely chopped blanched almonds
Candied cherries, halved
Candied orange peel strips

In large mixer bowl combine *1¹/₂ cups* of the flour and the yeast. Heat milk, the 6 tablespoons butter, the ¹/₃ cup sugar, and salt till warm (115° to 120°), stirring constantly. Add to dry mixture in bowl; add eggs. Beat at low speed with electric mixer for ¹/₂ minute, scraping bowl constantly. Beat 3 minutes at high speed. By hand, stir in enough of the remaining 2 cups flour to make a moderately soft dough.

Knead dough on lightly floured surface 8 to 10 minutes or till smooth and elastic. Place in a greased bowl; turn once to grease surface. Cover; let dough rise in warm place 1 to 1¹/₂ hours or till double. Punch down; turn out on lightly floured surface. Roll dough to a 20x12-inch rectangle. Brush with the 2 tablespoons melted butter.

Combine the 2 tablespoons sugar and the cinnamon; toss with the ¹/₂ cup chopped almonds and mixed fruits and peels. Sprinkle over dough. Roll as for jelly roll, beginning at long side; seal edge. Bring ends together to form a ring and place, seam side down, on greased baking sheet; pinch ends together to seal ring. Flatten slightly. Make slashes at intervals around edge. Cover; let rise in warm place 30 to 45 minutes or till almost double. Bake in 375° oven for 25 to 30 minutes. Cool slightly.

Combine powdered sugar, vanilla, and enough milk to achieve spreading consistency; spread over ring. Sprinkle with the 2 tablespoons almonds; decorate with candied cherries and orange peel. Makes 1 ring.

Shown from front: *Rosca de Reyes* for Epiphany, *Pan de Muerto* for All Souls' Day (see page 80) and *Pan Dulce.*

Pan de Muerto All Souls' Day Bread (photo on page 79)

1 **package active dry yeast**
¹/₃ **cup warm water (110°)**
¹/₂ **cup butter** *or* **margarine**
¹/₄ **cup granulated sugar**
¹/₂ **teaspoon salt**
3 **cups all-purpose flour**
1 **tablespoon orange-blossom**
   water *or* **water**
1 **teaspoon aniseed, crushed**
¹/₂ **teaspoon finely shredded**
   orange peel
2 **eggs**
1 **egg yolk**
1 **egg white**
2 **teaspoons water**
   Pink sugar *or* **granulated sugar**

Soften yeast in the ¹/₃ cup water; set aside. In mixer bowl cream butter, ¹/₄ cup sugar, and salt. Blend in ¹/₂ *cup* of the flour, the orange-blossom water, aniseed, and orange peel. Add eggs and egg yolk; beat 2 minutes at medium speed. Blend in yeast mixture and *1 cup* of the remaining flour; beat 3 minutes at high speed. By hand stir in remaining 1¹/₂ cups flour. Cover;refrigerate 4 hours or overnight.

Turn onto lightly floured surface. Remove ¹/₄ of the dough and set aside. Shape remainder into a ball. Place on greased baking sheet; flatten to a 6-inch round.

Divide reserved piece of dough into 4 portions. Roll two pieces into two 7-inch ropes to form "crossbones." Combine egg white and 2 teaspoons water. Place crossbones in an X atop loaf, attaching with some of egg white mixture.

Roll one of the remaining portions into a 2-inch ball. Make a 2-inch-wide indentation in center of loaf; place ball of dough in depression, attaching with egg white. Cut the last piece of dough into 4 portions; shape each into a teardrop and secure onto sides of loaf with egg white.

Cover and let rise in warm place 30 to 40 minutes or till nearly double. Bake in 325° oven for 35 to 40 minutes or till done. Remove to rack. Brush hot loaf with remaining egg white mixture; sprinkle with sugar. Repeat brushing and sprinkling after 5 minutes. Makes 1 loaf.

About this recipe: The literal translation of *Pan de Muerto* is "bread of the dead." Despite its forbidding connotation, the loaf is traditional fare for the November 2nd religious celebration, All Souls' Day. On this day, families honor departed relatives by visiting their graves, and this rich, brioche-like bread is served. You can omit the crossbones and teardrops, but don't miss this bread just because of its name.

Bolillos Spindle Rolls (photo on page 70)

7 **to 7¹/₄ cups all-purpose flour**
2 **packages active dry yeast**
2¹/₂ **cups water**
1 **tablespoon sugar**
1 **tablespoon salt**
1 **tablespoon shortening**
   Yellow cornmeal
1 **egg white**
1 **tablespoon water**

In large mixer bowl combine *3 cups* of the flour and the yeast. Heat the 2¹/₂ cups water, sugar, salt, and shortening just till warm (115° to 120°), stirring constantly to almost melt shortening. Add to dry mixture. Beat at low speed with electric mixer for ¹/₂ minute, scraping bowl. Beat 3 minutes at high speed. By hand, stir in enough of remaining 4¹/₄ cups flour to make a soft dough.

Knead on floured surface 10 to 12 minutes or till smooth. Shape into ball. Place in greased bowl; turn once to grease surface. Cover; let rise 1 to 1¹/₂ hours or till double.

Punch down; divide in 18 pieces. Cover; let rest 10 minutes. Shape each piece of dough into an oval 5 inches long. Pull and twist ends slightly. Place on greased, cornmeal-sprinkled baking sheets. Make lengthwise cut ¹/₄ inch deep on top of each. Beat egg white and 1 tablespoon water just till foamy; brush tops and sides of rolls. Cover; let rise about 1 hour or till double. Bake in 375° oven for 20 minutes. Brush again with egg white mixture. Bake 10 to 15 minutes longer or till golden brown. Makes 18.

Bizcochos Egg Biscuits

3 cups all-purpose flour
2 tablespoons sugar
4 teaspoons baking powder
1 teaspoon salt
1/2 cup shortening
2 slightly beaten eggs
2/3 cup milk

In a bowl stir together flour, sugar, baking powder, and salt. Cut in shortening till it resembles coarse crumbs. Measure *2 tablespoons* of beaten egg; set aside. Combine remaining egg and milk. Make a well in center of dry ingredients. Add egg-milk mixture all at once. Stir quickly with fork just till dough follows fork around the bowl.

Turn dough onto lightly floured surface (dough should be soft). Knead gently 10 to 12 strokes. Roll or pat dough 3/8 inch thick. Cut with 2- to 2 1/2-inch biscuit cutter. Place biscuits on ungreased baking sheet. Brush tops with reserved egg. Bake in 425° oven 14 to 15 minutes. Makes about 18.

Empanadas Dessert Turnovers

3 cups all-purpose flour
2 teaspoons baking powder
1/2 teaspoon salt
1/2 cup lard *or* shortening
2 eggs
1/2 cup milk
Pumpkin Filling
Fat for deep-fat frying (optional)
Powdered sugar *or* granulated sugar

Stir together flour, baking powder, and salt. Cut in lard or shortening till mixture resembles cornmeal. Beat eggs with milk. Add to flour mixture, stirring till combined (use hands if necessary).

Form dough into a ball; cover and chill 1 hour. Divide dough into 16 portions. On lightly floured surface roll each part to a 6-inch circle. Place about 3 tablespoons Pumpkin Filling on each. Moisten edges with a little water; fold in half, pressing edges with a fork to seal. Fry *or* bake as directed below. Makes 16.

To fry: Fry empanadas, a few at a time, in deep hot fat (375°) for about 4 minutes or till golden, turning once. Drain on paper toweling. Sprinkle with powdered sugar.

To bake: Place empanadas on baking sheet. Brush tops with a little milk; sprinkle with granulated sugar. Bake in 400° oven for about 15 minutes or till golden brown.

Pumpkin Filling: Stir together one 16-ounce can *pumpkin,* 1 cup packed *dark brown sugar,* 3/4 cup chopped *walnuts,* 1/2 cup *raisins,* 1 teaspoon ground *cinnamon,* and 1/4 teaspoon ground *cloves.* Makes about 3 cups.

For another filling: Well-drained crushed pineapple makes a tasty filling too. You will need about 3 cups, measured after draining, to fill 16 empanadas.

Churros Mexican Crullers (photo on page 70)

1 cup water
1 tablespoon sugar
1 teaspoon salt
1 cup all-purpose flour
2 eggs
Peel of 1/2 lemon
Fat for deep-fat frying
Granulated sugar *or* powdered sugar

In saucepan bring water, sugar, and salt to boiling. Remove from heat. Stir in flour all at once and beat till smooth. Beat in eggs one at a time until mixture is smooth. Spoon batter into pastry bag fitted with large star point. Pipe 3-inch strips onto waxed paper or floured surface. Add lemon peel to deep fat and heat to 375°. Fry churros, a few at a time, for 3 to 4 minutes or until golden brown, turning as necessary. Drain on paper toweling. Roll in granulated sugar or powdered sugar. Makes 24.

Huevos Reales *Royal Eggs*

6 egg yolks
2 tablespoons water
1/8 teaspoon salt
3/4 cup water
1/2 cup sugar
1/4 cup raisins
2 inches stick cinnamon
2 tablespoons light rum
Toasted slivered almonds
  (optional)

In small mixer bowl beat egg yolks, the 2 tablespoons water, and salt about 6 minutes or till thick and light. Turn into buttered 8x4x2-inch loaf pan; set in 13x9x2-inch pan on oven rack. Pour hot water 1 inch deep into outer pan. Bake in 350° oven 20 to 25 minutes or till set. Cover and chill.

Loosen egg mixture from sides of pan; turn out and cut into bite-size cubes. Place in serving bowl. In 1 1/2-quart saucepan combine the 3/4 cup water, sugar, raisins, and cinnamon; cover and simmer for 5 minutes. Remove from heat; discard cinnamon. Stir in rum; pour over egg cubes in bowl. Chill; sprinkle with almonds. Makes 5 servings.

Polvorones *Mexican Wedding Cakes*

1 cup butter *or* margarine
1/2 cup sifted powdered sugar
1 teaspoon vanilla
2 cups all-purpose flour
1/2 cup finely chopped pecans
1/8 teaspoon salt
Powdered sugar

Cream butter, the 1/2 cup powdered sugar, and vanilla. Combine flour, pecans, and salt. Stir into butter mixture. Shape dough in 1-inch balls. Place on ungreased baking sheet. Bake in 325° oven 20 to 25 minutes till lightly browned. Roll warm cookies in powdered sugar. Cool on wire racks, then roll again in powdered sugar. Sprinkle with additional chopped pecans, if desired. Makes 36.

Buñuelos *Fried Sugar Tortillas*

3/4 cup milk
1/4 cup butter *or* margarine
2 beaten eggs
3 cups all-purpose flour
1 teaspoon baking powder
1 teaspoon salt
Fat for frying
Anise Syrup

In saucepan heat milk and butter to boiling; cool. Stir in beaten eggs. Stir together flour, baking powder, and salt; add egg mixture and mix well. Knead dough on lightly floured surface 2 to 3 minutes till smooth. Shape into 20 balls. Let rest 5 minutes. Roll each ball into a 4-inch circle. Fry in deep hot fat (375°) about 4 minutes or till brown, turning once. Drain on paper toweling. Drizzle with Anise Syrup. Makes 20.

Anise Syrup: In saucepan bring 1 cup *piloncillo* or packed *dark brown sugar,* 1 cup *water,* and 1 tablespoon *aniseed* to a full boil. Reduce heat; boil gently, uncovered, 10 to 15 minutes or till syrup is thick. Strain. Makes 3/4 cup.

Sopaipillas *Fried Biscuit Puffs*

2 cups all-purpose flour
1 tablespoon baking powder
1/2 teaspoon salt
1 tablespoon shortening
2/3 cup lukewarm water
Fat for frying
Honey *or* sugar and cinnamon

Stir together flour, baking powder, and salt. Cut in the shortening till mixture resembles cornmeal. Gradually add the water, stirring with a fork (dough will be crumbly).

Turn onto floured surface; knead into a smooth ball. Divide dough in half; let stand 10 minutes. Roll each half into a 12 1/2x10-inch rectangle. Cut into 2 1/2-inch squares (do not reroll or patch dough). Fry a few at a time in deep hot fat (425°) till golden. Drain on paper toweling. Serve with honey or roll in sugar-cinnamon mixture. Makes 40.

Shown, front to back, are *Huevos Reales,* a regal egg dessert; *Polvorones,* nutty tea cakes; and *Buñuelos.*

Almendrado Almond Pudding with Custard Sauce

1 **cup sugar**
1 **envelope unflavored gelatin**
1¼ **cups water**
5 **egg whites**
¼ **teaspoon almond extract**
 Red food coloring
 Green food coloring
⅓ **cup finely chopped blanched almonds**
5 **slightly beaten egg yolks**
3 **tablespoons sugar**
 Dash salt
1½ **cups milk**
¼ **teaspoon vanilla**
 Blanched whole almonds (optional)

In saucepan combine 1 cup sugar and gelatin; add water. Cook and stir till gelatin dissolves. Chill till partially set. In large mixer bowl combine gelatin mixture, egg whites, and almond extract; beat at high speed about 5 minutes or till very light. Remove 1 cup mixture; tint pink. Turn into 6-cup tower mold; chill 10 minutes.

Divide remaining mixture in half. Tint one half green; stir chopped almonds into remaining mixture. Turn almond mixture into mold atop pink layer. Chill 10 minutes. Add green layer. Cover and chill several hours or overnight.

Meanwhile, in saucepan combine egg yolks, the 3 tablespoons sugar, and salt. Add milk; cook and stir, till sauce coats metal spoon. Remove from heat; stir in vanilla. Cover surface with waxed paper or plastic wrap; chill. Unmold gelatin onto platter; top with blanched whole almonds. Serve with the custard sauce. Makes 8 servings.

Postre de Virrey Viceroy's Dessert

½ **cup granulated sugar**
½ **cup water**
8 **beaten egg yolks**
½ **teaspoon ground cinnamon**
½ **cup dry sherry *or* orange juice**
½ **teaspoon vanilla**
8 **egg whites**
¼ **teaspoon cream of tartar**
1 **cup whipping cream**
2 **tablespoons powdered sugar**
16 ½**-inch slices sponge cake *or* pound cake**
½ **cup apricot jam**
 Chocolate shot
 Small multi-colored decorative candies

In 1-quart saucepan boil granulated sugar and water to thread stage (230° on candy thermometer). Pour syrup into top of double boiler; cool. Stir in egg yolks and cinnamon. Cook and stir over boiling water (upper pan should not touch water) for 10 to 15 minutes or till thick. Remove from heat and stir in sherry or orange juice and vanilla.

Beat egg whites with cream of tartar to soft peaks. Whip cream with powdered sugar till stiff. Fold whipped cream into egg whites.

Spread eight of the cake slices with apricot jam; top with remaining cake slices. Cut in cubes. Arrange *half* the cake cubes in a deep serving dish. Follow with *half* the egg yolk mixture and *half* the cream mixture. Repeat layers ending with cream. Cover and chill for 3 to 4 hours. Just before serving, sprinkle with chocolate shot and decorative candies. Makes 12 servings.

About this recipe: You may recognize *Postre de Virrey* as a variation of Trifle. *Pastel Esponjoso* is just the right size for making this elegant dessert.

Pastel Esponjoso Sponge Cake Loaf

1 **cup sifted cake flour**
1¼ **cups sifted powdered sugar**
5 **egg yolks**
½ **teaspoon salt**
5 **egg whites**
1 **teaspoon vanilla**
½ **teaspoon cream of tartar**
½ **teaspoon almond extract**

Combine flour and ½ *cup* of the powdered sugar; set aside. Beat egg yolks about 5 minutes or till thick and lemon-colored. Gradually add remaining ¾ cup powdered sugar and salt, beating constantly. With clean beaters, beat egg whites, vanilla, cream of tartar, and almond extract till soft peaks form. Gently fold yolk mixture into egg whites.

Sift flour mixture over batter ⅓ at a time; gently fold in after each addition. Turn into an *ungreased* 9x5x3-inch loaf pan. Bake in 325° oven for 45 to 50 minutes. Invert cake in pan; cool. Makes 1 loaf.

Almond-flavored and almond-crowned *Almendrado* looks like a fluffy green,
white, and pink cloud. A delicate custard sauce is spooned over each heavenly serving.

Flan *Caramel Custard*

1/3 **cup sugar**
2 **eggs**
1 **13-ounce can evaporated milk**
    (1²/₃ cups)
1/4 **cup sugar**
1 **teaspoon vanilla**
    Dash salt

In small skillet heat and stir the 1/3 cup sugar over medium heat till sugar melts and becomes golden brown. Quickly pour caramelized sugar into a 3-cup ring mold, tilting mold to coat bottom and sides.

In bowl beat eggs; stir in milk, the 1/4 cup sugar, vanilla, and salt. Pour into caramel-coated mold. Set mold in baking pan on oven rack. Pour hot water around mold in pan to a depth of 1 inch. Bake, uncovered, in 325° oven for 50 to 55 minutes or till a knife inserted halfway between center and edge comes out clean. Chill.

Carefully loosen custard from sides and center; invert on platter. Makes 4 to 6 servings.

Leche Quemada *Caramel Milk Pudding*

1 **14-ounce can *sweetened***
    ***condensed* milk**
    Coffee liqueur
    Unsweetened whipped cream

Pour milk into 8x1½-inch baking dish; cover with foil. Place in shallow pan; pour boiling water around it to depth of ¾ inch. Bake in 425° oven for 1 hour. Serve warm or cold. Top with coffee liqueur and cream. Serves 4 to 5.

Budín de Plátano y Piña Banana and Pineapple Pudding

2 whole eggs
2 egg yolks
2 cups milk
¼ cup sugar
3 tablespoons rum
10 ladyfingers *or* 6 thin slices
      pound cake
1 large banana, peeled and sliced
      (1 cup)
1 8¼-ounce can pineapple
      chunks, well drained
2 egg whites
¼ cup sugar

In 1½-quart saucepan beat whole eggs and egg yolks. Stir in milk and the first ¼ cup sugar. Cook and stir over medium-low heat about 10 minutes or till mixture is slightly thickened and coats a metal spoon. Remove from heat; stir in rum. Chill.

Line bottom and sides of a well-buttered 1½-quart soufflé dish with ladyfingers or pound cake, cutting pieces as needed to fit. Arrange banana and pineapple over cake. Pour chilled custard over fruit.

Beat egg whites to soft peaks. Gradually add the remaining ¼ cup sugar, beating to stiff peaks. Cover pudding with meringue. Bake in 325° oven 12 to 15 minutes or till meringue is golden. Serve warm or chilled. Makes 8 servings.

Helado de Mango Mango Sherbet

1 cup water
½ cup sugar
   Dash salt
2 mangoes, peeled and sliced
½ cup light cream
¼ cup lemon juice
2 egg whites
¼ cup sugar

In saucepan combine water, the ½ cup sugar, and salt. Cook 5 minutes; cool. In blender container combine mangoes and cream. Cover; blend till smooth. (Or, mash mangoes with fork and stir in cream.) Stir in cooled syrup and lemon juice. Freeze in one 6-cup or two 3-cup refrigerator trays till partially frozen.

Beat egg whites to soft peaks; gradually add the ¼ cup sugar, beating to stiff peaks. Turn frozen mixture into chilled mixer bowl; break into chunks. Beat smooth. Fold in beaten egg whites. Return to cold tray; freeze firm. Makes 6 to 8 servings.

Dulce de Naranja Orange Candy

3 cups sugar
¼ cup boiling water
1 cup evaporated milk
¼ teaspoon salt
½ cup chopped pecans
1 tablespoon grated orange peel
1 teaspoon grated lemon peel

In heavy saucepan over low heat melt *1 cup* sugar to a rich brown color. Blend in water; stir to dissolve sugar. Blend in remaining 2 cups sugar, milk, and salt. Bring to a boil; cook, covered, 3 minutes. Reduce heat to low; cook, uncovered, without stirring to soft ball stage (238° on candy thermometer). Cool without stirring to 110°. Fold in pecans and peels. Beat till creamy; pour into a buttered 8x8x2-inch pan. Cool; cut in squares. Makes about 24 pieces.

Dulce con Nueces Brown Sugar Pralines

2 cups packed dark brown sugar
1 cup light cream
2 tablespoons butter *or* margarine
2 cups pecan halves *or* pieces

In 2-quart saucepan combine sugar and cream; mix well. Bring to boiling over medium heat, stirring constantly. Cook and stir to soft ball stage (238°). Remove from heat; add butter. Stir in pecans. Beat about 1 minute or till candy just begins to lose its gloss. Drop by tablespoons onto waxed paper, shaping into patties with back of spoon. If the candy becomes too stiff to drop, add a little hot water to make the right consistency. Makes 24 pieces.

Cocada *Coconut Custard*

½ cup sugar
½ cup water
3 inches stick cinnamon, broken up
1 3½-ounce can flaked coconut
3 cups milk
4 eggs
¼ teaspoon vanilla
½ cup whipping cream
2 tablespoons toasted sliced almonds (optional)

In uncovered 2-quart saucepan simmer sugar, water, and cinnamon for 10 minutes. Strain; discard cinnamon pieces. Add coconut; cook, uncovered, about 5 minutes or till syrup is nearly absorbed, stirring frequently. Stir in 2½ *cups* of the milk; cook till mixture is hot. In bowl beat eggs with remaining ½ cup milk. Stir about *1 cup* of the hot mixture into egg mixture; return to saucepan. Cook and stir till mixture thickens slightly but does not boil. Stir in vanilla. Turn into a 1½-quart bowl or individual serving dishes; chill. Whip cream; mound onto pudding. Garnish with almonds. Makes 8 to 10 servings.

Capirotada *Bread Pudding*

2 cups water
1½ cups packed dark brown sugar
¾ teaspoon ground cinnamon
2 tablespoons butter *or* margarine
6 slices toast
½ cup raisins
½ cup pine nuts *or* chopped almonds
2 apples, peeled, cored, and sliced (2 cups)
½ cup shredded monterey jack cheese (2 ounces)

In medium saucepan bring the water, brown sugar, and cinnamon to boiling; reduce heat and simmer, uncovered, 3 minutes. Stir in butter. Cut toast in 1-inch pieces; fold into the sugar mixture along with raisins and nuts.

Place *half* of the mixture in bottom of 8x8x2-inch square baking dish, top with apples, then remaining toast mixture. Cover and bake in 350° oven for 20 minutes. Uncover and sprinkle with cheese. Bake, uncovered, 20 minutes more or till apples are tender. Serve warm with light cream, if desired. Makes 6 servings.

Tamales de Dulce *Sweet Tamales*

Cornhusks, aluminum foil, *or* parchment
4½ cups Masa Harina tortilla flour
2⅔ cups warm water
1½ cups lard *or* shortening
¾ cup sugar
1 teaspoon salt
½ teaspoon ground cinnamon
1 cup raisins
1 cup chopped mixed candied fruits and peels
¼ cup chopped almonds *or* pine nuts

Soak cornhusks in warm water several hours or overnight to soften. Pat with paper toweling to remove excess moisture. (Or, use 8x6-inch squares of foil or parchment.)

Mix tortilla flour and 2⅔ cups water; let stand 20 minutes. Meanwhile, in large mixer bowl beat together lard, sugar, salt, and cinnamon till fluffy. Beat in flour mixture till well combined. Mix raisins, fruits and peels, and nuts.

Measure ¼ cup of the flour mixture onto each tamale wrapper; spread to a 5x4-inch rectangle, having one long edge of dough at edge of wrapper and leaving equal spaces at the ends (use pictures on page 15 as a guide).

Spoon 2 tablespoons of the fruit-nut mixture onto dough about one inch in from the long edge, bringing the filling out to both ends. Roll tamales jelly-roll fashion starting with the edge nearest filling and being sure to make a tight roll. Tie ends securely with pieces of cornhusk or string (for foil, fold ends under or twist to seal).

Place tamales on rack in steamer or electric skillet. Add water to just below rack level. Bring to boiling; cover and steam over medium heat 1½ hours or till tamale pulls away from wrapper. Add more water as needed. Makes 18.

For a different filling: You can use 1½ teaspoons fruit preserves or jam to fill each tamale.

Bebidas *Beverages*

Sangría *Red Wine Punch*

2 oranges
2 lemons
2 fifths rosé, burgundy, *or other* red wine (1.5 liters)
1/4 cup sugar
1/4 cup brandy (2 ounces)
1 apple
1 28-ounce bottle carbonated water, chilled

Chill *one* orange and *one* lemon for garnish. Squeeze juice from the second orange and lemon. Place juices, wine, sugar, and brandy in a large pitcher or bowl. Stir to dissolve sugar; chill. Just before serving, divide mixture into 2 pitchers or pour into punch bowl. Cut chilled orange into wedges. Slice chilled lemon into cartwheels. Core apple and cut in wedges. Thread fruit on 2 long skewers to stand in pitchers or float fruit in punch bowl. Slowly add chilled carbonated water. Makes about 24 (4-ounce) servings.

Refresco Regio *Royal Refreshment*

2 oranges, peeled
1 medium pineapple, peeled, cored, and cut in chunks *or* 1 20-ounce can pineapple chunks, drained
2 cups strawberries, halved
2 fifths dry white wine, chilled (1.5 liters)
3/4 cup brandy (6 ounces)
1/2 cup sugar
1/4 cup lemon juice
2 cups carbonated water, chilled

Section oranges over a bowl to catch juice; reserve juice. Arrange orange sections, pineapple chunks, and strawberry halves in a single layer on shallow baking pan; freeze. In a punch bowl stir together the reserved orange juice, the chilled wine, brandy, sugar, and lemon juice till sugar dissolves. Before serving, add fruits and chilled carbonated water. Makes 18 to 20 (4-ounce) servings.

Margaritas en Jarra *Pitcher Margaritas*

2 cups crushed ice
3/4 cup tequila (6 ounces)
1/3 cup lime juice
1/4 cup powdered sugar
1/2 of an egg white (1 tablespoon)
1/2 ounce Triple Sec (1 tablespoon)
Lime slices

In blender container combine the crushed ice, tequila, lime juice, powdered sugar, egg white, and Triple Sec. Cover and blend till very frothy. Transfer to pitcher; garnish with lime slices. Serve in salt-rimmed cocktail glasses. Makes 6 (4-ounce) servings.

To prepare glasses: Rub the rim of each cocktail glass with a little *lime juice.* Invert glass in a shallow dish of *salt;* shake off excess salt.

Rompope *Rich Cooked Eggnog*

3 cups milk
3/4 cup sugar
8 egg yolks
1 cup rum *or* brandy
1/2 teaspoon vanilla
Ground cinnamon

In large saucepan combine milk and sugar; bring to boiling. Reduce heat and simmer for 5 minutes, stirring occasionally. Meanwhile, beat egg yolks about 6 minutes till thick and lemon-colored. Gradually stir about *1 cup* of the hot milk mixture into egg yolks. Return egg mixture to saucepan. Cook and stir over low heat about 3 minutes more or till thickened. Cool to room temperature, stirring occasionally. Stir in rum or brandy and vanilla; chill. Serve in small glasses, sprinkle with a little ground cinnamon, if desired. Makes 12 (4-ounce) servings.

Sip *Margaritas en Jarra* from salt-rimmed glasses, or for delightful wine punches enjoy *Sangría* or *Refresco Regio.*

Sangrita Tomato-Chili Cocktail

6 **fully ripe tomatoes, peeled, seeded, and cut up** *or* 1 **28-ounce can tomatoes**
1 **cup orange juice**
1 **4-ounce can green chili peppers, rinsed and seeded**
1 **slice of a medium onion**
1/3 **cup lime juice**
1 **teaspoon sugar**
1/4 **teaspoon salt**
   Bottled hot pepper sauce
   Tequila

In blender container place *undrained* tomatoes, orange juice, chili peppers, onion, lime juice, sugar, and salt. Cover and blend till smooth. Add bottled hot pepper sauce to taste. Chill tomato mixture.

Serve each person 1/2 *cup* chilled tomato mixture and 1 to 2 ounces (2 to 4 tablespoons) tequila in small separate glasses. Makes 8 to 10 servings.

Tequila Madrugada Tequila Sunrise

1/3 **cup orange juice**
1 1/2 **ounces tequila (3 tablespoons)**
1 **teaspoon grenadine**

Combine orange juice, tequila, and grenadine; pour over ice in tall glass. Makes 1 serving.

Coctel Bandera Mexicana Mexican Flag Cocktail

1 **small jicama**
6 **seedless green grapes**
6 **maraschino cherries**
1/4 **cup sugar**
1/4 **cup lime juice**
1 **cup tequila (8 ounces)**
   Crushed ice

With a melon baller cut 6 balls from the jicama. Skewer one grape, one jicama ball, and one cherry on each of 6 picks or small skewers. Stir together sugar and lime juice. Add tequila; mix well. Pour over crushed ice in 6 cocktail glasses; garnish with the skewered fruit. Makes 6 servings.

About this recipe: The skewered fruits represent the green, white, and red of the Mexican flag. If you can't buy jicama, use apple or banana pieces dipped in lemon juice.

Spirits of Mexico

Besides abundant fruit juices, coffee, and chocolate, Mexico boasts several unique alcoholic beverages. You may be familiar with *tequila,* a harsh, clear liquor distilled from the *agave* or century plant. Similar to tequila, but made in a different region, is *mezcal.* Aged tequila, smoother and amber in color, is known as *añejo.* Mexicans also ferment the sap of the *agave* to make *pulque.* Very common in Mexican markets, *pulque* is rarely found in the United States. However, Mexican beers *(cervezas)* and wines are favorite accompaniments to hot Mexican food.

To drink tequila Mexican-style, hold a lime wedge in the left hand while balancing some salt in the curve between the thumb and first finger. In the right hand, hold a glass of tequila. Then, quickly lick the salt, drink the tequila, and suck the lime. (For a more cautious approach, sip *Margaritas en Jarra,* page 88.)

Chocolate Mexicano Mexican Hot Chocolate (photo on page 71)

6 **cups milk**
1/2 **cup sugar**
3 **squares (3 ounces)**
    unsweetened chocolate,
    cut up
1 **teaspoon ground cinnamon**
1/4 **teaspoon salt**
2 **beaten eggs**
2 **teaspoons vanilla**
    Stick cinnamon (optional)

In saucepan combine milk, sugar, chocolate, ground cinnamon, and salt. Heat and stir till chocolate melts and milk is very hot. Gradually stir *1 cup* of the hot mixture into eggs; return to saucepan. Cook 2 to 3 minutes more over low heat. Remove from heat. Add vanilla; beat with rotary beater or *molinillo* till very frothy. Pour into mugs; garnish with cinnamon sticks. Makes 6 (8-ounce) servings.

About this recipe: A *molinillo* is a carved wooden beater that is twirled between the hands to make chocolate frothy (see photo on page 71).

Café de Olla Pot Coffee

6 **cups water**
1/2 **cup packed dark brown sugar**
4 **inches stick cinnamon**
2 **whole cloves**
1/2 **cup regular-grind coffee**

In coffeepot or saucepan combine water, brown sugar, cinnamon, and cloves. Bring to boiling, stirring till sugar dissolves. Add coffee; simmer, covered, for 1 minute. Stir; let stand about 5 minutes or till grounds settle. Strain into mugs. Makes 8 (6-ounce) servings.

Atole Hot Cornmeal Beverage

2 **cups milk**
1/4 **cup Masa Harina**
    tortilla flour
1/3 **cup sugar**
1/4 **teaspoon salt**
1/4 **teaspoon vanilla**
    Ground cinnamon *or* stick
    cinnamon

In saucepan stir together ½ *cup* of the milk, tortilla flour, and ½ cup *water*. Cook and stir over low heat till thickened and bubbly. Blend in remaining 1½ cups milk, sugar, salt, and vanilla; heat through. Serve hot atole in mugs; sprinkle with ground cinnamon or place a cinnamon stick in each mug. Makes 6 (4-ounce) servings.

About this recipe: Mexicans enjoy this thick, grainy beverage flavored with nuts, cinnamon, chocolate, or fruit.

Champurrado Chocolate Atole

1/4 **cup Masa Harina**
    tortilla flour
2/3 **cup packed dark brown sugar**
2 **squares (2 ounces)**
    unsweetened chocolate,
    cut up
1/2 **teaspoon ground cinnamon**

In saucepan combine tortilla flour and 3 cups *water*. Cook and stir over low heat till thickened and bubbly. Add sugar, chocolate, and cinnamon. Heat and stir till chocolate melts. Beat with a rotary beater or *molinillo* till frothy. Makes 6 (4-ounce) servings.

Agua de Tamarindo Tamarind Water

8 **ounces tamarind pods**
    (1½ cups)
3 **cups water**
1/3 **cup sugar**
    Ice

Remove and discard as much of the outer rind of the tamarind pods as possible. Wash pods; break or cut into small pieces. Place in saucepan; add water. Bring to boiling; reduce heat. Cover and simmer 10 minutes. Remove from heat; cool. Cover and chill several hours or overnight. Strain and discard tamarind; stir sugar into liquid till dissolved. Pour over ice. Makes about 4 (4-ounce) servings.

Glossary

Achiote: Annatto seeds, used for seasoning and coloring (page 9)

Adobo: A sauce made with vinegar, chilies, and other seasonings (pages 53, 63)

Almuerzo: Late breakfast or brunch (page 20)

Antojito: Spanish word for "little whim," a name for appetizers and snacks (pages 24-29)

Atole: A thick, grainy beverage made with masa (page 91)

Burrito: Large flour tortilla wrapped around a filling (page 44)

Cazuela: Earthenware casserole (page 58)

Cena: Late supper (page 20)

Cerveza: Mexican beer (page 90)

Chiles: Chili peppers (pages 10-11)

Chimichanga: Fried burrito (page 44)

Chorizo: Spicy Mexican sausage (pages 8, 18)

Cilantro: Fresh coriander leaves (page 9)

Comal: Round griddle used to bake tortillas

Comida: Main meal of the day, eaten in the afternoon (page 20)

Desayuno: Light breakfast (page 20)

Enchilada: Tortilla with filling and sauce (pages 46-47)

Epazote: A Mexican herb (page 9)

Escabeche: Pickle or marinade

Frijoles: Spanish word for beans (page 8)

Guacamole: Sauce made of seasoned, mashed avocados (page 17)

Hominy: A form of corn (page 8)

Jícama: Crisp root vegetable (page 8)

Masa: Dough made from ground corn; used to make tortillas, tamales, and atoles (page 8)

Masa Harina tortilla flour: Dried masa flour (page 8)

Merienda: Snack or light supper in late afternoon (page 20)

Mezcal: Distilled liquor made from the century plant (page 90)

Mole: Concoction or sauce made with chilies (pages 48, 58, 59)

Molinillo: Carved wooden beater used to prepare hot chocolate (pages 71, 91)

Nacho: Appetizer made with chilies, cheese, and tortilla chips (page 26)

Nopal: Edible pad of a cactus (page 8)

Olla: An earthenware pot (page 49)

Panucho: A stuffed, fried tortilla (page 45)

Pepitas: Pumpkin seeds (pages 8, 29)

Piloncillo: Hard cone of dark brown sugar (page 8)

Plantain: A variety of hard green banana, always eaten cooked

Pulque: Fermented sap of the century plant (page 90)

Relleno: A filling or a stuffed poblano chili (pages 18, 69)

Salsa: Spanish word for sauce; also the name for a specific table sauce (pages 16-17)

Sopa seca: "Dry soup"—a starchy casserole served as a separate course at comida (page 73)

Taco: A tortilla wrapped or folded around a filling; may be crisp or soft (pages 13, 40, 41)

Tamales: Corn-based breads, often filled with meat or sweets, and steamed (pages 14-15, 87)

Tamarind: A fruity pod (page 8)

Tequila: Distilled liquor made from the century plant (page 90)

Tomatillos: Green husk tomatoes (page 8)

Tortilla: Thin pancake made of masa or wheat flour (pages 12-13); also an omelet (page 66)

Tostada: A flat, fried tortilla topped with assorted fillings (page 42)

Index